APA 7th Manual Made Easy: Full Concise Guide Simplified for Students

Updated for the APA 7th Edition

Student Citation Styles Series

Appearance Publishers
2021

APA 7th Manual Made Easy: Full Concise Guide Simplified for Students Updated for the APA 7th Edition

Student Citation Styles Series
Book 1

"APA 7th Manual Made Easy" was written specifically for the updated edition of the American Psychological Association Publication Manual (APA 7th edition) and includes 80+ examples of different kinds of references.

Revised according to the 7th edition of the APA Manual, this guide is offering general format and examples of paper layout, title page, abstract, contents, headings, in-text citations, quotations, reference list, footnotes, lists, tables and figures, notes, appendices, etc. among others including APA student paper sample and APA professional paper sample. Learn more about writing style, language, and formatting.

This student guide reflects the newest version of the APA Manual and will address the vast majority of questions about using APA 7th edition correctly with 80+ examples of references.

Table of Contents

Thank you for the purchase!

Do you enjoy reading?

As a thank-you, we are happy to give you some free goodies…

Get Your

FREE

Extra

follow the link:

https://appearancepublishers.wordpress.com/apa-manual-made-easy/

to get your FREE extra

Your support is much appreciated and we are looking forward to hearing your thoughts on your purchase!

FOREWORD

APA (The American Psychological Association)

This student guide reflects the newest version of the *American Psychological Association (APA) Publication Manual* (7th edition), which was released in October 2019.

Revised according to the 7th edition of the APA manual, this guide is offering examples on:

- General format of APA papers,
- In-text citations,
- Reference list,
- Footnotes,
- Tables/figures,
- Appendices,

including:

- APA student paper and
- APA professional paper samples.

This student guide will assist you to learn how to use the American Psychological Association (APA) Style for references and citations.

This guide will address the vast majority of questions about using APA style correctly. However, if you are working on a complex document or if you require more information on specific area of APA Style, please consult the *Publication Manual of the American Psychological Association* (7th edition) or the APA Style website (https://apastyle.apa.org) for more details.

If you are a student, consult with your professor to find out what style your discipline requires prior to choosing APA Style for formatting your work.

Keep in mind: your instructor is the final authority on how to format your paper correctly.

Appearance Publishers
2021

1.0 APA INTRODUCTION

Referencing is acknowledging the copyrights of resources used in your academic writing, which gives all necessary information to identify the work cited within the text.

APA (*American Psychological Association*) style provides clear guidelines for writing academic papers regardless of chosen subject and/or discipline, however, it is most commonly used to format papers within the social sciences.

There are 2 main segments in the APA referencing style:
1. In-text citations and
2. Their corresponding references listed at the end of paper.

Any source that you have used and referred to in your academic writing must be:
1. Acknowledged in text (as in-text citation),
2. Included in reference list (as full reference).

As a rule, APA is most often used for the following disciplines:

- Social Sciences:
  - Psychology,
  - Sociology,
  - Linguistics,
  - Criminology,
- Business,
- Nursing.

Advantages of using APA style:

1. APA style allows readers to understand writer's ideas quickly by providing a well-known structure throughout the paper.
2. Abiding by APA's standards permits readers to focus on paper's content rather than get distracted by unfamiliar formatting.

2.0 IMPORTANT CHANGES IN THE 7TH EDITION

The American Psychological Association (APA) updated manual includes the following changes:

- The requirements for researchers and student have changed,
- The importance of bias-free language has increased,
- Online sources citing has become more common.

This chapter highlights the most important differences between the previous and the latest editions.

For more details concerning changes, please consult the APA Publication Manual (7th edition).

2.1 Writing Style

The most important changes relate to pronoun usage:

- The APA manual advises to use "they" as a singular pronoun or for a person whose gender is irrelevant:

OLD:	Student's success depends on what he or she did while studying.
NEW:	Student's success depends on what they did while studying.

- To refer to linguistic examples, use double quotation marks instead of italics:

OLD:	While using the singular pronoun *they*
NEW:	While using the singular pronoun "they"

2.2 Language

The APA manual has updated guidelines to bring writing about age, gender, and ethnic identity in line with best practices:

- Use "person-first" language:

OLD:	A disabled…
NEW:	A person with a disability…

- Use descriptive phrases to label group of people instead of using adjectives as nouns:

OLD:	The blind…
NEW:	People who are blind…

- Use specific labels instead of general ones:

OLD:	Asian Americans…
NEW:	Chinese Americans…

- Use exact age ranges instead of broad categories:

OLD:	People under 30 years old…
NEW:	People in the age range of 20 to 30 years old…

2.3 Formatting

General

APA manual determines different formatting requirements for student and professional papers:
1. Papers for credit in a course,
2. Papers for scholarly publication.

- APA manual has increased flexibility for choosing fonts:
  - Times New Roman - 12pt,
  - Calibri - 11pt,
  - Georgia - 11pt,
  - Arial - 11pt, etc.

The APA manual recommends different title pages for student papers and professional papers:
- For student papers, running head is no longer a requirement,
- For professional papers, running head must be included on every page:
    o "Running head:" label is no longer used:

| OLD: | Running head: ANALYSIS OF WELFARE POLITICS IN JAPAN |
| NEW: | ANALYSIS OF WELFARE POLITICS IN JAPAN |

Student paper title page includes:
- A page header:
    o Page number flush right,
- The title of the paper,
- The name of each author of the paper,
- The institutional affiliation for each author,
- The course name and number:
    o Use the format used by the institution:
        ▪ Example: LIT 2012,
        ▪ Example: GOV 101,
- The instructor's name and title:
    o Use the instructor's preferred form:
        ▪ Example: Dr. Anderson,
        ▪ Example: Ms. Tyler,
- The assignment's due date:
    o Use the most common format:
        ▪ Example: March 4, 2021,
        ▪ Example: 4 March 2021,

Professional paper title page includes:
- A page header:
    o Running head with the page number,
- The title of the paper,
- The name of each author of the paper,
- The affiliation for each author,
- The author note (if applicable).

Heading Levels

Headings are used to structure the material and guide the reader through the text.

The APA updated manual has changed level 3, level 4, and level 5 headings to improve readability:

- All headings are:
  - Bold,
  - Title Case,
- Headings differ by the use of:
  - Italics,
  - Indentation.

	6th Edition APA Headings (OLD)	*7th Edition APA Headings (NEW)*
Level 1	**Centered, Bold, Title Case Headings** Text starts with a new paragraph.	**Centered, Bold, Title Case Heading** Text starts with a new paragraph.
Level 2	**Flush left, Bold, Title Case Heading** Text starts with a new paragraph.	**Flush left, Bold, Title Case Heading** Text starts with a new paragraph.
Level 3	**Indented, bold, lowercase with a period.** Text continues on the same line/paragraph as the heading.	***Flush Left, Bold, Italic, Title Case Heading*** Text starts with a new paragraph.
Level 4	***Indented, bold, italic, lowercase with a period.*** Text continues on the same line/paragraph as the heading.	**Indented, Bold, Title Case Heading With a Period.** Text continues on the same line/paragraph as the heading.
Level 5	*Indented, italic, lowercase with a period.* Text continues on the same line/paragraph as the heading.	***Indented, Bold, Italic, Title Case Heading With a Period.*** Text continues on the same line/paragraph as the heading.

2.4 In-Text Citations

APA 7 manual has set the following rule for in-text citations:
- Any sources with 3+ authors (three and more authors) are now referred to using the name of the first author followed by "et al.":

OLD:	(Wilson, Anderson, Thomas, & Taylor, 2012)
NEW:	(Wilson et al., 2012)

- APA guidelines describe how to format quotations from research participants:
  - Simply indicate that the quotation is from a research participant in the very text. There is no need to provide a reference list entry.

2.5 Reference List

Most important updates regarding reference list are:

- For sources with several authors, up to 20 authors' names must be listed in a reference list entry.
- For sources with 20+ authors, after the first 19th authors, any additional authors' names are replaced with an ellipsis (…) followed by the final listed author's name. Do not use an ampersand (&) before the final author's name:

OLD:	Martinez, V. W., Garcia, S. R., Lopez, T. H., Thomas, T. V., Taylor, H. B., Martin, N. N., . . . Davis, W. X. (1999).
NEW:	Martinez, V. W., Garcia, S. R., Lopez, T. H., Thomas, T. V., Taylor, H. B., Martin, N. N., Moore, G. L., Roberts, R. E., Walker, E. R., Hall, H. L., Rivera, P., Gonzalez, W. L., Perez, S., Campbell, G. H., Green, G., Rivera, E. H., Hill, J. L., Baker, D. D., Torres, B., . . . Davis, W. X. (1999).

- The publisher location for books is no longer included in the reference list entry:

OLD:	Jones, M. D. (2011). *The muse is music: Jazz poetry from the Harlem Renaissance to spoken word* (Vol. 104). Illinois: University of Illinois Press.
NEW:	Jones, M. D. (2011). *The muse is music: Jazz poetry from the Harlem Renaissance to spoken word* (Vol. 104). University of Illinois Press.

- Digital object identifiers (DOIs) and URLs are now presented as hyperlinks (https://) for electronic sources.
- The label "DOI:" is no longer used for references entries:

OLD:	doi: 10.1096/2340867208.2012.4739274
NEW:	https://doi.org/10.1096/2340867208.2012.4739274

- The label "Retrieved from" is only used when a retrieval date is provided. Instead, include the website name:

OLD:	Forbes, C. (2021, March 18). APA citation style, 7th edition: New & notable changes [Blog post]. Retrieved from https://libguides.ecu.edu/c.php?g=982594&p=7316507
NEW:	Forbes, C. (2021, March 18). APA citation style, 7th edition: New & notable changes. *Libguides.* https://libguides.ecu.edu/c.php?g=982594&p=7316507

2.6 Tables and Figures

- Tables and figures are now formatted in parallel; they use consistent rules for titles and notes.
- Tables and figures may be presented either:
  - In the text of the paper or
  - In appendices.

3.0 GENERAL GUIDELINES

3.1 Paper Layout

APA manual has the following requirements for the paper layout:
- Standard paper, A4 format:
  - 8.5 inches x 11 inches,
- 1-inch margins on all sides,
- Page header at the top of every page:
  - For a professional paper, this includes your paper title and the page number.
  - For a student paper, this only includes the page number.
- Standard font:
  - Times New Roman - 12pt.,
  - Georgia - 11pt.,
  - Arial - 11pt., etc.
- Double-spaced text,
- The first line of every paragraph should be indented 0.5 inches.

3.2 Page Header (Running Head)

The page header is the text line that appears at the top of every page:
- For student paper, the header contains only the page number flush right.
- For professional paper, the header consists of the running head and the page number flush right.

The running head is a shortened version of the paper's title that appears at the top of every page:
- The running head should contain no more than 50 characters.

For student paper, to create a page header:	**For professional paper,** to create a page header:

1. Insert the page number, flush right.	1. Insert shortened title of the paper flush left, all capital letters:
	    ○ The title should be up to 50 characters in length and take only 1 line of text,
	    ○ Abbreviate long titles if needed.
	 2. Insert the page number, flush right.

Example (for student paper):
1

3.3 Fonts

APA manual recommends using standard available fonts:
- Serif fonts:
  - Times New Roman - 12pt.,
  - Georgia - 11pt., etc.
- Sans serif fonts:
  - Arial - 11pt.,
  - Calibri - 11pt., etc.

3.4 Major Paper Sections

Any APA-formatted research paper should include 4 major sections:
1. Title page,
2. Abstract,
3. Main body,
4. References.

3.4.1 Title Page / Cover Page

APA manual provides different requirements for formatting the title page / cover page for:
1. Student papers:
   - Intended for credit in a course,
2. Professional papers:
   - Intended for scholarly publication.

Student paper title page includes:	**Professional paper title page** includes:
1. A page header, 2. The title of the paper, 3. The name of each author of the paper, 4. The institutional affiliation for each author, 5. The course name and number, 6. The instructor's name and title, 7. The assignment's due date.	1. A page header, 2. The title of the paper, 3. The name of each author of the paper, 4. The affiliation for each author, 5. The author note (if applicable).

	Student Paper Title Page Elements	**Professional Paper Title Page Elements**
General	All text should be double-spaced	
Header	Page number flush right at the top of the page	Running head with the page number flush right at the top of the page
Title	Title should be placed in the upper half of the page: • Title case, bold, centered • Title can take up to 2 lines	

Author(s)	The author's name includes first name, middle initials, and last name:
	• Do not use titles or degrees
	• List all the authors in order of contribution
	• For 2 authors, separate the names with "and":
	  o Laura L. Hernandez and Dennis Wilson
	• For 2+ authors, separate the names with commas and "and" for the last author's name:
	  o Laura L. Hernandez, Dennis Wilson, John Lee, and Mia K. Anderson	

Author's Affiliation	Indicate the institution or location where the author conducted the research	
Course	Use the format used by the institution: Example: LIT 2012 Example: GOV 101	-
Instructor	Use the instructor's preferred form: Example: Dr. Anderson Example: Ms. Thomas	-
Assignment Due Date	Use the most common format: Example: March 4, 2021 Example: 4 March 2021	-

Author Note		-	An author note should appear in the bottom half of the page:
			• "Author note" is bold and centered
			• The paragraphs are left-aligned
			• The first line of each paragraph is indented 0.5 inches
			
			Author note is divided into 4 paragraphs:
			
			The 1st paragraph includes:
			  o The author's name
			  o The ORCID iD symbol
			  o The URL for the ORCID iD
			
			The 2nd paragraph indicates:
			  o Any change in affiliation
			  o Any deaths of the authors
			
			The 3rd paragraph includes:
			  o Disclosure of conflicts of interest
			  o Acknowledgment of financial and other support
			  o Study registration
			
			The 4th paragraph includes:
			  o Contact information

General Format:

1

Full Title of Paper:

Following Title

First and Last Name (Author)

Department, University (Affiliation)

Course Code: Course Name (Course)

Dr. Professor's Name (Instructor)

Month Day, Year (Due Date)

Example:

Modern Period in the English Literature:

Key Points about Modern Period

Marcus White

Department of English Literature, Heldens University

ELD 1201: Modern English Literature

Dr. Korsh

April 25, 2021

General Format:

Full Title of Paper:

Following Title

First and Last Name(s) (Authors)

Department, University (Affiliations)

Author Note

1st Author's Name, the symbol for the ORCID iD, https://orcid.org/####-####-####

2nd Author's Name, the symbol for the ORCID iD, https://orcid.org/####-####-####

...

Any change in affiliation or any deaths of the authors.

Disclosures or acknowledgments

Contact information for the corresponding author.

Example:

Modern Period in the English Literature:

Key Points about Modern Period

Marcus White and White Andrew

English Literature Online Lab

Department of English Literature, Heldens University

Author Note

Marcus White ⦿ https://orcid.org/1257-8436-2456

White Andrew ⦿ https://orcid.org/4678-8926-3324

White Andrew is now at the Department of English History, Heldens University.

We have no conflicts of interests to disclose.

Correspondence concerning this article should be addressed to White Andrew, 34 E New Heldens St., North Hollick KB 302928. Email: whiteandrew@heldens.edu.

3.4.2 Abstract

The abstract is a 150-250-word concise summary of the key points of your paper:
- Begin the abstract on a separate page after the title page.
- Center and bold the label "Abstract".
- Your abstract should:
  - Be double-spaced,
  - Be single not indented paragraph,
  - Contain no more than 250 words.

Content

- Abstract should contain at least:
  - Research topic and questions,
  - Methods and results,
  - Data analysis,
  - Findings,
  - Conclusions.
- Additionally, you may:
  - Include possible implications of your research.
  - List paper's keywords:
    - Indent the first line 0.5 inches after the abstract paragraph.
    - Italicize "Keywords:".
    - Add 3-5 keywords in lowercase letters, not italicized, separated with commas.
    - Do not use a period after the final keyword.

Example:

2

Abstract

Lorem ipsum dolor sit amet, consectetur adipiscing elit. Vivamus id dapibus libero. Phasellus vel urna nisi. Orci varius natoque penatibus et magnis dis parturient montes, nascetur ridiculus mus. Curabitur ac luctus nisi, sed maximus nibh. Curabitur congue accumsan nisi, a sollicitudin turpis aliquam at. Phasellus suscipit est eget augue sagittis risus eu, auctor lorem. Donec sit amet libero nisi. Pellentesque sit amet ante rutrum, feugiat ipsum vel, ornare leo. Proin tincidunt purus ut massa aliquam, fermentum malesuada elit interdum. Sed posuere ut mauris non molestie. Integer nec condimentum mi, nec ornare nisi. Nulla non sagittis nibh. Suspendisse in felis at ipsum tristique pharetra sed in neque. Cras orci purus, pulvinar non placerat id, dapibus sed felis.

    Keywords: Ipsum, purus, pulvinar

3.4.3 Table of Contents

APA manual does not provide guidelines for formatting the table of contents:
- The table of contents is not a required part of paper and should only be included if instructed:
  - The table of contents should appear on a separate page between the abstract and main body.
  - Label "Contents" at the top of page:
    - Bold,
    - Centered.
  - List the headings with respective page numbers:
    - Include all level 1 and level 2 headings:
      - Other heading levels are optional.
    - Indent different heading levels to ease reading.

Example:

3

Contents

3.5 Headings

Headings are used to guide the reader through the text:
- The title of the paper is considered to be level 1 heading.
- Use the same font and spacing for all headings as for the text.
- Do not use letters or numbers for headings.
- Do not add extra lines above or below headings.
- Do not label introduction section with a heading:
  - For subsection in the introduction section, use level 2 heading.

There are 5 heading levels in APA:

Level 1

Centered, Bold, Title Case Heading
Text starts with a new paragraph.

Level 2

Flush left, Bold, Title Case Heading
Text starts with a new paragraph.

Level 3

Flush Left, Bold, Italic, Title Case Heading
Text starts with a new paragraph.

Level 4

   Indented, Bold, Title Case Heading With a Period. Text continues on the same line/paragraph as the heading.

Level 5

   Indented, Bold, Italic, Title Case Heading With a Period. Text continues on the same line/paragraph as the heading.

Example:

Method (Level 1)

…
Study (Level 2)
…
Participants (Level 2)
…
Men (Level 3)
…
Women (Level 3)
…

Results (Level 1)

…
Ability (Level 2)
…
First Results (Level 3)
…

    Men in Black. (Level 4) …
    Assistants. (Level 5) …
    Men in White. (Level 4) …
    Assistants. (Level 5) …
    Women in Black. (Level 4) …
    Assistants. (Level 5) …
    Women in White. (Level 4) …
    Assistants. (Level 5) …
Second Results (Level 3)
…

    Men in Black. (Level 4) …
    Men in White. (Level 4) …
    Women in Black. (Level 4) …
    Women in White. (Level 4) …
Disability (Level 2)
…

Special headings are used for certain sections of a paper and are always positioned at the top of the new page, bold and centered:
- Abstract,
- Contents,
- Title of Paper,
- References,
- Footnotes,
- Appendix.

3.6 Lists

For lists with a specific order, use Arabic numerals followed by a period:
- Numbered list should contain full sentences or paragraphs instead of phrases:
  - The first word of each sentence or paragraph should be capitalized.
  - Each sentence or paragraph should end with a period.

Example:
1. Sentence(s) / Paragraph. 2. Sentence(s) / Paragraph. 3. Sentence(s) / Paragraph.

For lists without a specific order, use bullets:
- Bulleted list should contain full sentences or paragraphs instead of phrases:
  - The first word of each sentence or paragraph should be capitalized.
  - Each sentence or paragraph should end with a period.

Example:
• Sentence(s) / Paragraph. • Sentence(s) / Paragraph. • Sentence(s) / Paragraph.

For seriation within sentences, use letters in brackets (a, b, c, …).

Example:
Accessibility and convenience include (a) the broad variety of products and services; (b) online comparison; (c) adequate buildings; (d) basic and urban infrastructure services; (e) proffered location; (f) public amenities; (g) centralized and smart home system; (h) comfort and security.

Points can be also separated with bulleted list:
- If bulleted list is a part of the sentence, treat it accordingly:
  - Maintain standard sentence capitalization and punctuation.

Example:

Accessibility and convenience include
    • the broad variety of products and services;
    • online comparison;
    • adequate buildings;
    • basic and urban infrastructure services;
    • proffered location;
    • public amenities;
    • centralized and smart home system;
    • comfort and security.

3.7 Numbers and Statistics

3.7.1 Numbers

Write numbers from 0 to 9 in words:
- One,
- Two,
- Three,

Write numerals for 10 and higher:
- 10,
- 14,
- 356,
- 1334.

You should always use Arabic numerals (1...9) instead of Roman numerals (I...IX):
- For numbers greater than 1,000, separate groups of three digits with commas except:
  o Page numbers,
  o Temperatures,
  o Acoustic frequencies, and
  o Binary code.
- Do not add apostrophes to plurals of numbers:
  o The 30s,
  o The 2000s.

Write a numeral for:
- A number 10 and higher,
- A number right before a unit of measurement:
  o 2 kg,
  o 55 ml,
- A number indicating:
  o Time,
  o Date,
  o Age,
  o Money amount,
- A number indicating:
  o Mathematical functions,
  o Percentages,
  o Ratios.

Write a number in words for:
- A number from 0 to 9 (except above-mentioned cases),
- A number that is a common fraction:
  o One half,
  o Two thirds,
- A number that begins a sentence.

Combine numerals and words in any order when numbers are written next to each other to avoid confusion:

- 2 three-year-old sons,
- Two 3-year-old sons.

Decimal Fractions

- For numbers less than 1, a leading 0 is optional before the decimal point:
  - If the variable can be greater than 1, use a leading 0:
    - $x = 0.36$ ml.
  - If the variable cannot be greater than 1, do not use a leading 0:
    - $x = .055$ ml.

Ordinal Numbers

- You can decide whether to use a superscript or not, but keep the same format throughout the paper:
  - 2nd participant,
  - 2nd participant.

3.7.2 Statistics

Statistical symbols guidelines:

- Words are preferred to symbols in the text,
- For mathematical symbols = and +, use the symbols,
- Currency and percentage symbols should only be used with numerals,
- Vector and matrix symbols should be written in bold,
- All other statistical symbols should be written in italics.

For statistics, any data should be presented in:

- The text (for less than 3 numbers),
- Tables (for 4-20 numbers),
- Figures (for more than 20 numbers).

3.7.3 Mathematics

- Simple equations can be written in a regular line of text.
- All equations should be numbered sequentially:
  - The equation number should be displayed in parentheses on the same line of the equation towards the right margin of the page.
- Any equation should be referred to by its number in the text:
  - Equation 3 …,
  - The third equation …
- For mathematical expressions, use spaces between elements:
  - $x^2 + y^2 = z^2$.
- Subscripts come first and are followed by superscripts:
  - x_1^2.
- Use a slash (/) for fractions.

Example:	
$$x^2 + y^2 = z^2$$	(1)

3.8 Tables and Figures

Tables and figures are optional visuals for the paper to structure the information and ease readers' understanding:
- Tables are any graphics that use rows and columns to structure the content.
- Figures are any visuals other than tables.

3.8.1 General Guidelines

- Number all tables sequentially.
- Number all figures sequentially.
- Each table and figure should be comprehensible without having to refer to the text:
  - Include explanation of every abbreviation.
- When citing the table or figure from another source, maintain the original structure.

3.8.2 Tables

Elements of Tables

- Numbers:
  - All tables should be numbered with Arabic numerals sequentially in the same order as they appear in the text:
    - Table 1,
    - Table 2, etc.
  - Numbers are bolded and left-aligned.
- Titles:
  - The title of the table should be written in italicized title case below the number of the table.
  - Leave a blank line between the number and the title of the table.
- Headings:
  - All columns must have headings.
  - All headings should be written in sentence case.
- Body:
  - Short entries should be centered, sentence case.
  - Longer entries should be sentence case.
  - Leave cell blank if data were not obtained:
    - Put a dash in cell and a general note if needed to explain why the cell is blank.
- Spacing:
  - Use double spacing for:
    - The number of the table,
    - The title of the table,
    - Notes.
  - Use single, one and a half, or double spacing for:
    - The body of the table.

- Borders:
  - Spacing and alignment are usually enough to determine the cells:
    - Avoid using many horizontal lines,
    - Do not use any vertical lines,
  - Include only horizontal lines that are needed for clarity to separate:
    - Column spanners,
    - Elements of a decked head,
    - Totals, etc.
  - Do not use:
    - Vertical lines,
    - Borders around each cell.
- Notes:
  - Notes should supplement the content of the table and can be of the following types:
    1. General,
    2. Specific,
    3. Probability notes.
  - Notes should appear in the above-mentioned order below the table:
    - General notes provide citations or any additional information for the table in regards to units of measurement, symbols, abbreviations, etc.
    - Specific notes explain certain column, row, or element.
    - Probability notes clarify statistical significance of specific values.

Tables Checklist

1. Is the table necessary?
2. Is the table number bold and left-aligned?
3. Is the table title italicized title case and left-aligned?
4. Does every column have a column heading? Are column headings centered?
5. Does the table use correct spacing?
6. Are entries in the left column left-aligned beneath the centered stub heading?
7. Are all other column headings and cell entries centered?
8. Are all abbreviations and special symbols explained?
9. Are the table notes in general, specific, and probability order, double-spaced, and left-aligned?
10. If the table is from another source, is it properly cited?
11. Are all tables numbered with Arabic numerals sequentially?
12. Are all tables referred to in the text?
13. Are all tables mentioned in the text in the same order as they appear in the paper?

Lorem ipsum dolor sit amet, consectetur adipiscing elit. Nam aliquam odio et arcu cursus lobortis. Curabitur commodo ipsum ac ullamcorper hendrerit. Phasellus volutpat urna in gravida dictum. Phasellus vitae nulla ligula.

Table 2

Title of Table Title Case

Stub Heading	Column Spanner 1		Column Spanner 2	
	Column Heading 1	Column Heading 2	Column Heading 3	Column Heading 4
	Table Spanner 1			
Row 1	XXX	XXX[a]	XXX	XXX
Row 2	XXX	XXX	XXX	XXX
	Table Spanner 2			
Row 3	XXX	XXX	XXX***	XXX
Row 4	XXX	XXX	XXX***	XXX

Note. A general note.

[a]A specific note.

***A probability note.

Proin cursus massa urna, porttitor placerat turpis hendrerit vel. Mauris non sem viverra, suscipit purus vel, vulputate velit. Sed tellus quam, ultricies a cursus a, euismod non leo. Class aptent taciti sociosqu ad litora torquent per conubia nostra, per inceptos himenaeos.

3.8.3 Figures

Figures include all graphical information other than tables:
- Graphs and charts,
- Images and photos,
- Maps, etc.

Elements of Figures

- Numbers:
  - o All figures should be numbered with Arabic numerals sequentially in the same order as they appear in the text:
    - Figure 1,
    - Figure 2, etc.
  - o Numbers are bolded and left-aligned.
- Title:
  - o The title of the figure should be written in italicized title case below the number of the figure.
- Spacing:
  - o The number and title of figure should be double spaced.
- Image (figure itself):
  - o The image of the figure is positioned under the title.
  - o The image of the figure should be of legible size and resolution.
  - o Maintain consistent size of fonts:
    - Between 8 and 14 pt.
  - o For headings and axis, use title case capitalization.
  - o For descriptions, use sentence case capitalization.
- Legends:
  - o The legends should be written in title case.
  - o The legends should go within or under the image.
- Notes:
  - o Notes should supplement the content of the figure and can be of the following types:
    1. General,
    2. Specific,
    3. Probability notes.
  - o Notes should appear in the above-mentioned order below the figure:
    - General notes provide citations or any additional information for the figure in regards to units of measurement, symbols, abbreviations, etc.
    - Specific notes explain certain elements.
    - Probability notes clarify statistical significance of specific values.

Pellentesque imperdiet diam ligula, aliquam laoreet ante faucibus ut.. Aenean varius eros a nibh sagittis, id mattis diam rhoncus. Vestibulum maximus tincidunt metus ac congue.

Figure 2

Title of Figure Title Case

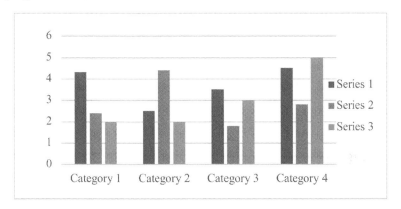

Note. General note explaining units of measurement, abbreviations, etc. or provide citation information.

Aenean ac felis eget magna dignissim sodales. Suspendisse imperdiet nisl et nisi condimentum pharetra. Proin vitae tellus semper, venenatis quam in, lobortis libero. Quisque tristique mauris fringilla ornare vehicula. Duis a odio erat.

Figures Checklist

1. Is the figure necessary?
2. Is the figure number bold and left-aligned?
3. Is the figure title italicized title case and left-aligned? Is the title descriptive of the content?
4. Are all elements of the figure clearly labeled?
5. Are all abbreviations and special symbols explained?
6. Is the figure's legend written in title case?
7. Are the figure notes in general, specific, and probability order, double-spaced, and left-aligned?
8. If the figure is from another source, is it properly cited?
9. Are all figures numbered with Arabic numerals sequentially?
10. Are all figures referred to in the text?
11. Are all figures mentioned in the text in the same order as they appear in the paper?
12. Are parallel figures prepared according to the same scale?

3.8.4 Notes

There are 3 types of notes for tables and figures:
1. General,
2. Specific,
3. Probability notes.

- **General notes** provide citations or any additional information for the table or figure in regards to units of measurement, symbols, abbreviations, etc.

Example:
Note. The respondents were asked to indicate those events that they considered to be the most traumatic events. Adapted from *An Insider's Guide to a Big 5*, by F. Miller, 2018, p. 14. Copyright 2019 by Simon & Schuster. SL = Satisfaction level.

- **Specific notes** explain a particular column, row, or certain entry in the table or certain value in the figure:
  - Use superscript lowercase letters (a, b, c, …) to provide specific notes.

Example:
[a] Two participants failed to fill in the survey.   [b] $f = 45$.

- **Probability notes** clarify certain values for statistical significance.

Example:
* $p < .01$.   ** $p < .02$.

3.8.5 Referring to Tables and Figures in the Text

Refer to tables and figures by their numbers:
- Avoid referring to tables and figures by their positions or content:

INCORRECT:	The table on page 23 shows... As can be seen in the image below... The photograph of a vase is a great example of...
CORRECT:	Table 2 shows... As can be seen in Figure 2... Figure 1 is a good example of...

Highlight or analyze data from table and figure instead of restating the information which is clearly shown in the very table and/or figure:
- Avoid redundant statements from tables and figures in the text:

INCORRECT:	As Table 1 shows, there are 450 girls in School 1, 350 girls in School 2, and 290 girls in School 3...
CORRECT:	Table 1 indicates a notable preponderance of girls in example schools...

4.0 IN-TEXT CITATIONS

The APA manual suggests that writers should use:
- The past simple tense or
- The present perfect tense.

Example:
Brown (2019) found… Brown (2019) has found…

Alternatively, if writing does not require traditional forms writer are still allowed to use:
- The present simple tense.

Example:
Brown (2019) finds…

4.1 Basics

Parenthetical and Narrative Citation

The in-text citation can be of 2 forms:
1. Parenthetical and
2. Narrative.

Parenthetical Citation

Example:
According to recent research… (Taylor, 2018).

Narrative Citation

Example:
Taylor (2018) notes that…

Author-Date Method

The author-date method should be followed for all in-text citation when using APA:
- The author's last name and the year of publication should always appear in the text:
  - (Martin, 2013).
- Page number of the used source may be omitted in the text in case you refer to a general idea from another work rather than directly quoting the material.
- Page number must be included in the citation when directly quoting the material:
  - Use the abbreviation "p." (for one page) or "pp." (for several pages) before including the page number(s).
  - Use a dash for page range:
    - (Perez, 2017, p. 199),
    - (Perez, 2017, pp. 199–201).
- Each source mentioned in the text must be listed in the reference list and vice versa.

Titles of Sources within the Text

- If you refer to the title of a source in the text, capitalize all words that are 4+ letters long:
  - *Wonder and Hope.*
- Capitalize short words that are nouns, verbs, pronouns, adjectives, and adverbs:
  - *Lighting New Horizon,*
  - *There is Hope to Love.*
- Capitalize both words in a hyphenated compound word:
  - *Broad-Minded Person.*
- Capitalize the first word after a dash or colon:
  - "Gendered Labor Migration: The Case of Indramayu Regency."
- If the title of the source is italicized in your reference list, italicize it and use title case capitalization when referring to the source in the text:
  - *The Real Home,*
  - *The Crown,*
  - *Moxie.*
- If the title of the source is not italicized in your reference list, use double quotation marks and title case capitalization when referring to the source in the text:
  - "The Balmoral Test."

4.2 Short Quotations

When directly quoting from a source, include:
1. The author,
2. Year of publication, and
3. Page number.

- Start the quotation with a signal phrase that includes the author's last name and the date of publication in parentheses (in brackets). Page number should be placed after the quotation (in brackets):

Example:
According to Harris (2018), "the anticipated benefits relate to the purchaser's judgment concerning product quality and ability of the commodity or service to perform certain tasks" (p. 29).

- Alternatively, the author's last name, the year of publication, and the page number can be placed in parentheses after the quotation (in brackets).

Example:
He stated, "The anticipated benefits relate to the purchaser's judgment concerning product quality and ability of the commodity or service to perform certain tasks" (Harris, 2018, p. 29), but she did not offer an explanation as to why.

4.3 Long Quotations (Blockquotes)

Direct quotations that are 40+ words long should be placed in a free-standing block. Quotation marks are omitted:
- Do not add extra blank line before/after the quotation.
- Start the quotation on a new line, indented 0.5 inch from the left margin.
- The entire quotation should be typed on the new margin and indented 0.5 inch.
- Double-space the entire quotation.
- The parenthetical citation should be placed after the punctuation mark.

Example:

Pellentesque imperdiet diam ligula, aliquam laoreet ante faucibus ut. Duis diam lectus, malesuada non sollicitudin id, pellentesque at diam. Phasellus convallis urna eget augue ullamcorper fringilla. Sanchez's (2019) study found the following:

In September 2017, a Brexit debate was held at the Society's Annual General Meeting to discuss the process of Brexit and how it might affect the lives of microbiologists. The Society's General Secretary, Professor Maggie Smith, was joined by Professor Graeme Reid, Chair of the Campaign for Science & Engineering, who is a member of the Government's High Level Forum on Science and Brexit; and Professor Nick Talbot, a mycologist from the University of Exeter, who sits on the Russell Group's Europe Advisory Group, which is in direct contact with the Brexit negotiators both from the UK side and the EU side. (p. 340)

4.4 Quotations from Sources without Pages

For the sources which do not have pages, you may reference another logical element (or a combination of elements) for the direct quotation to help readers find the cited part, such as:
- A paragraph,
- A chapter,
- A table, etc.

Example:

Lewis (2010) defined globalization as the spread of free-market capitalism to all parts of the world (paras. 6–7).

… (Carroll, 2017, Table 2)
… (Bains, 2002, 03:26)

4.5 Summary or Paraphrase

- Page numbers may be omitted when referring to a general idea of another work or paraphrasing another author's material. Include only the author and year of publication in your in-text reference:

Example:
According to Okoye (2018), globalization can be explained as an intensification of social relations worldwide through the linkage of distant localities.

- When paraphrasing there are 3 ways to place the citation within your text:
  - o Citation at the beginning,
  - o Citation in the middle,
  - o Citation at the end.

Citation at the Beginning

Example:
Nwaigwe (2018) stated that China is the second-largest trading partner of the United States after the EU…

Citation in the Middle

Example:
…the second-largest trading partner of the United States after the EU (Nwaigwe, 2018), while the U.S. is the largest for China.

Citation at the End

Example:
…partner of the United States after the EU, while the U.S. is the largest for China (Nwaigwe, 2018).

4.6 Making Changes to Direct Quotes

Generally, a direct quotation should not be altered. However, in order to integrate the quote into the work, sometimes the changes are needed:

- As long as the meaning of the quote remains the same, the writer may:
  - o Shorten quotes,
  - o Clarify quotes,
  - o Add emphasis to quotes,
  - o Fix errors in quotes.

Shortening Quotes

- Use an ellipsis (. . .) with a space before and after omitted words, phrases, or sentences to indicate that some part of the quote has been left out:

Example:

According to Thierfelder (2017), "other than making sure the economic interactions in the region are active and peaceful . . . the Silk Road will also act as an economic and infrastructure incentive" (p. 73).

Clarifying Quotes

- Use square brackets ([]) for adding a word, phrase, or sentence to clarify any unclear part of the quote:

Example:

In the view of Brakman (2008), "the [Senate election] results are in sync with states' presidential votes" (p. 56).

Adding Emphasis to Quotes

- When emphasizing a word, phrase, or sentence in a quote, *italicize it* and include the words [emphasis added]:

Example:

In the view of Brakman (2008), "the results reflected *local patterns* [emphasis added]" (p. 56).

Fixing Errors in Quotes

- Highlight a spelling or grammatical error with the Latin word [*sic*], italicized and put in square brackets, put directly after the error:

Example:

In the view of Havranekova (2012), "the creation of a shorter journey by the use of high-speed railwayses [*sic*]" (p. 39).

4.7 General Format

When referring to another author's work in the text use the following general format for an in-text citation.

General Format:
(Author, Year, p. #). (Author, Year, pp. #–#).

The symbol # should be replaced by the page number.

4.8 Examples

1 Author

Example:
Research by Devarajan (2019) supports... (Devarajan, 2019)

2 Authors

- If the work has 2 authors, name both authors each time you refer to the source:
  - Use the word "and" between the authors' names mentioned in the text.
  - Use the ampersand (&) in parentheses.

Example:
Research by Lakatos and Robinson (2019) shows... (Lakatos & Robinson, 2019)

3+ Authors

- If the work has 3+ authors, name only the first author followed by "et al." each time you refer to the source:

Example:
(Lin et al., 2012) Lin et al. (2012) offered...

- If there are several works with the same first authors' names:
  - To avoid ambiguity, list as many first authors' names as needed followed by "et al." to clearly identify the reference by its corresponding in-text citation:

Example:	
If you reference 2 works of such authors:	*To avoid ambiguity, use the following examples for in-text citations:*
Nain, Okoye, Berthou, Jardet, and Szczerbowicz (2020)	(Nain, Okoye, Berthou, et al., 2020)
Nain, Okoye, Siena, Brakman, and Thierfelder (2020)	(Nain, Okoye, Siena, et al., 2020)

- As long as "et al." is plural, it should always replace 2+ authors' names:
    - If there is only one author's name left to replace with "et al.", write the author's name instead.

Organization as an Author

- If the author is an organization, replace the author's name with the organization name for an in-text citation and treat the organization as the author:

Example:
According to the American Psychological Association (2019),...

- If the organization has an abbreviation, add the abbreviation in square brackets after the full organization name the first time the source is referred and then use only the abbreviation in following citations:

Example:	
First citation:	(American Civil Liberties Union [ACLU], 2014)
Second citation:	(ACLU, 2014)

Unknown Author

- When the source does not have an author, refer to the work by its full or shortened title instead of author's name:
    - Titles of books and reports should be italicized.
    - Titles of articles, chapters, and web pages should be put in quotation marks.

Example:
Other than making sure the economic interactions in the region are active and peaceful the Silk Road will also act as an economic and infrastructure incentive ("Making Changes," 2016).

- APA manual suggests to treat "Anonymous" as the author's name and use the name "Anonymous" as the author in the reference list as well:
    - (Anonymous, 2001).

- If no date of publication is known, use the abbreviation "n.d." (no date) instead of date:

Example:
The nurses also plan referrals, discharge process and do follow-ups to facilitate the success of the treatment processes ("Heart Care," n.d.).

2+ Works in the Same Parentheses

- If you refer to 2+ works by different authors within a single citation, order them alphabetically and separate them by a semi-colon.

Example:
(Boom, 2020; Code, 1999)

- If you refer to 2+ works by the same author within a single citation, give the author's name once and follow with dates:
  - Dates order: "No date" go first, then years, then "in-press".

Example:
(Yeung, n.d., 1999, 2018, in press)

Authors with the Same Last Names

- Use the author's initials along with the last name for in-text citation to prevent confusion. Separate citations by a semi-colon:

Example:
(E. Johnson, 2001; L. Johnson, 1998)

2+ Works by the Same Author in the Same Year

- If you have to cite 2+ sources by the same author in the same year, use lower-case letters (a, b, c, …) after the year to order the entries and prevent confusion:

Example:
Research by Guo (2013a) revealed weak possibility. However, another study (Guo, 2013b) resulted in…

- For person-to-person communication (interviews, letters, e-mails, etc.), cite the communicator's name, state that it is a personal communication, and include the full date of the conducted communication:
  - According to APA manual, personal communication should not be added to the reference list.

Example:

(S. Schultz, personal communication, January 12, 2021).

- A footnote can be used to reference personal communication as well:

Example:

[1] B. Virani also named other risk factors of the disease such as poor diet and smoking (personal communication, December 14, 2020).

Traditional Knowledge of Indigenous Peoples

- When citing information obtained from a person who was not a research participant, treat the citation as personal communication:
  - Include the person's full name, nation or Indigenous group, location, and any other relevant details before the "personal communication" and date of the citation:

Example:

(John Howlett, AC Testings, lives in New York, New York, personal communication, February 2021)

Electronic Sources

- Cite an electronic source the same way as any other source:

Example:

Grange (2013) showed...

Indirect Sources

- If you cite a source that was initially cited in another source, name the original source in a signal phrase:
  - Include the secondary source in the in-text citation with the words "as cited in".
  - Include the year of the original source in the in-text citation.

Example:
Cosman offered... (as cited in McAlister, 2016, p. 34).
(Cosman, 2001, as cited in McAlister, 2016, p. 34).

Sources without Page Numbers

- When a source does not have pages, include any other relevant element (or a combination of elements) that will help readers find the cited part:
  - A paragraph,
  - A chapter,
  - A table, etc.:

Example:
(Bacon, 1999, Chapter 6) (Cardiac Rehabilitation Registry section, 2008, para. 2) (Arthur, 2009, Slide 36)

4.9 Quick Summary

Author Type	Parenthetical Citation	Narrative Citation
1 author	(Parsons, 2021)	Parsons (2021)
2 authors	(Parsons & Grace, 2021)	Parsons and Grace (2021)
3+ authors	(Parsons et al., 2021)	Parsons et al. (2021)
Organization as an author	(Macmillan Dictionary, 2021)	Macmillan Dictionary (2021)
Abbreviated group author		
• First citation	(American Civil Liberties Union [ACLU], 2021)	American Civil Liberties Union (ACLU, 2021)
• Subsequent citations	(ACLU, 2021)	ACLU (2021)
Same author / same date	(Parsons, 2021a, 2021b)	Parsons (2021a, 2021b)
Same surname authors	(A. Parsons, 2021; B. Parsons, 2020)	Alan Parsons (2021) and Bella Parsons (2020)
Multiple works	(Heise, 2018; Port of Vancouver, 2017; Wee et al., 2021)	Wee et al. (2021), Heise (2018), and Ports of Vancouver (2017)

5.0 REFERENCE LIST

This chapter gives basic guidelines for formatting the reference list.

Reference List vs. Bibliography

A reference list includes only the sources you refer to in your writing.

A bibliography includes all the sources used during the research for background reading including those which were not mentioned in the text itself.

The purpose of creating the reference list is to let your readers find all the sources you used:
- All references cited in the text must appear in the reference list and vice versa:
    o Personal communications are not included in the reference list as long as they cannot be retrieved.

Do not include references for:
- Sources that you only consulted for background reading,
- General mentions of websites or periodicals,
- Personal communications,
- Common knowledge.

5.1 Formatting a Reference List

Reference list should appear on a separate page at the end of your paper:
- Label "References" in bold, centered, and at the top of the page.
- All references should be double-spaced.
- All lines after the first line of each entry should be indented 0.5 inch from the left margin (hanging indentation).
- Each source cited in the text must appear in reference list and vice versa.
References are ordered alphabetically by authors' last names:
- If the author is unknown, order the reference entry by the first word of the title ignoring articles "the", "a", and "an".

5.1.1 Authors

- All authors' names should be inverted (last names should go first).
- Authors' first and middle names should be written as initials.
- List up to 20 authors of a particular source:
    o Each author's name and initials should be separated from the next author with a comma.
    o Use an ampersand (&) before the last author's name.
    o If there are 21 or more authors, use an ellipsis (…) after the 19th author, and then the final author's name (with no ampersand).
- For several sources by the same author, list the entries in chronological order by the date of publication.

5.1.2 Titles

- For the titles of books, chapters, articles, reports, webpages, capitalize only:
    - The first letter of the first word of the title and subtitle,
    - The first word after a colon or a dash, and
    - Proper nouns.
- The titles of longer works should be italicized:
    - Books,
    - Collections,
    - Newspapers.
- The titles of shorter works should NOT be italicized:
    - Chapters in books,
    - Essays.

5.1.3 Articles in Academic Journals

- For the titles of articles capitalize only:
    - The first letter of the first word of the title and subtitle,
    - The first word after a colon or a dash, and
    - Proper nouns.
- Academic journal titles should be written in full and italicized:
    - Capitalize all major words in the titles of academic journals.
    - Leave any nonstandard punctuation and capitalization that is the original academic journal title:
        - *MediaGROUP* instead of *Mediagroup*,
        - *House & Garden* instead of *House and Garden*.

5.1.4 DOI or URL

- Works that can be accessed online should have a DOI or URL:
    - A DOI (digital object identifier) is an identification number that never changes and links reader to the document on the Internet.
    - A DOI is preferred over a URL.
    - Include the protocol (http:// or https://) for the DOI and URL:
        - DOI must always be presented in the format https://doi.org/xxxx.xxxx.xxxx
    - Do not add a period (.) after the DOI or URL.

5.1.5 Abbreviations in References

- Common parts of sources are abbreviated to save space in reference entries:

Revised edition	–	Rev. ed.
Second edition	–	2nd ed.
Editor / Editors	–	Ed. / Eds.
Translator / Translators	–	Trans. / Trans.
No date	–	n.d.
Page / Pages	–	p. / pp.
Paragraph	–	para.
Volume / Volumes	–	Vol. / Vols.
Number	–	No.

5.2 Author / Authors

The following guidelines apply to all kinds of sources listed in the reference list.

1 Author

- Author's last name, followed by author's initials (if any).

Example:
Garcia, H. (2019). *The boy who harnessed the wind.* Hachette Livre.

2 Authors

- List authors' last names, followed by initials.
- Separate authors' names with a comma.
- Use an ampersand (&).

Example:
Roberts, E. R., & Mitchell, G. N. (2014). Binary stars as the key to understanding planetary nebulae. *Nature Communications, 34*(5), 34-36. http://dx.doi.org/1024.3463.5540/x056k

3 to 20 Authors

- List authors' last names, followed by initials.
- Separate authors' names with a comma.
- The last author's name is preceded by ampersand.

Example:
Gray, E., Edwards, F. V., Stewart, A. T., Cook, G. H., & King, C. (2014). The concurrent emergence and causes of double volcanic hotspot tracks on the Pacific plate. *Nature Communications, 37*(2), 104-107. http://dx.doi.org/1124.3463.3544/xk7rs

20+ Authors

- Any reference entry should have no more than 20 authors' names in total.
- List authors' last names, followed by initials.
- Separate authors' names with a comma.
- After the first 19 authors' names, use an ellipsis (. . .) in place of the remaining authors' names.
- The last author's name is NOT preceded by ampersand.

Green, A., Collins, F., Wright, D., Collins, H., Miller, B., Reed, G., Morgan, F. L., Green, V.,
Anderson, C., Adams, D., Li, Q., Scott, R., Hernandez, T. K., Walker, C., Baker, A.
K., Evans, T. T. R., Morris, B. O., Brown, B., White, M., . . . Murphy, E. K. (2010).
Molecular mechanisms underlying the evolution of the signalosome. *Science
Advances, 54*(7), 22-26. http://dx.doi.org/1544.3463.4540/drky77

2+ Works by the Same Author

- Order several sources with the same author by the year of publication:
  - "n.d." comes first,
  - then dates (earliest one comes first),
  - then "in press".

Parker, R. T. (n.d.)...
Parker, R. T. (1999)...
Parker, R. T. (2012a)...
Parker, R. T. (2012b, May)...
Parker, R. T. (in press)...

- If the same author is a sole author of one work and is the first author of another group work, list the one-author entry first.

Campbell, N. H. (Ed.). (2015). *Methods for in vitro evaluating antimicrobial activity: A review.*
Houghton Mifflin Harcourt.
Campbell, N. H., & Edwards, E. Y. (Eds.). (2015). *Tunnelling spectroscopy of Andreev states
in graphene.* Pearson Education.

- For the references that have the same first author and different following authors, order the entries alphabetically.

Phillips, V. C., Campbell, S., Johnson, F. T., Hall, T. Y., & Lopez, H. (2017). The Rohingya
people of Myanmar: Health, human rights, and identity. *International Journal of
Clean Coal and Energy, 56*(8), 23-31.
Phillips, V. C., Rogers, F. L., Green, T. D., Baker, V., & Harris, D. D. (2017). Charting
organellar importomes by quantitative mass spectrometry. *International Journal of
Geosciences, 1*(2), 34-56.

2+ Works by the Same Author / Same Year

- For the references by the same author and published in the same year, check if there are more specific publication dates:
  - Works with only a year are listed before specific dates.
  - Order references with specific dates chronologically.
- If several references have the same publication date:
  - Order them alphabetically by the title coming after the date of publication.
  - Assign letters (a, b, c, …) to the year to avoid confusion when referring to the sources in the text.

Example:

Wright, F. R. (2015a). Branched-chain and aromatic amino acids in relation to behavioral

problems among young Inuit from Nunavik, Canada: A cohort study. *International Journal of Organic Chemistry, 7*(6), 8-12.

Wright, F. R. (2015b). Chemokine profiles of interstitial pneumonia in patients with

dermatomyositis: A case control study. *International Journal of Medical Physics, Clinical Engineering and Radiation Oncology, 12*(5), 6-7.

Group Author / Organization

- Group authors (referred to as "organization") can include:
  - Corporations,
  - Government agencies,
  - Organizations, etc.
- Treat the organization as the author's name and format the rest of reference as normal.
- Give the full name of the group author in your reference list:
  - Abbreviations may be used only in the text.

Example:

Canadian Oxford Dictionary. (2012). Heritage. In *Canadian Oxford Dictionary*. Houghton

Mifflin Harcourt.

Unknown Author

- If the source does not have an author, move the title of work to the place of author's name.
- Use "Anonymous" if the author of the work is signed as "Anonymous.".

Example:

New Oxford Dictionary of English (7th ed.). (2019). Oxford University Press.

- Use a shortened title of work when referring to the source without author in the text:
  - For example, in-text citation of the source given in example above would be: (New Oxford Dictionary, 2019).

5.3 Books

- APA manual requires DOIs for all books that have one (whether printed or digital).

General Format

General Format:
Author, A. A. (Year). *Title of book: Subtitle of book* (Edition). Publisher. DOI

Author, A. A.:
> List each author's last name and initials as Author, A. A., Author, B. B., & Author, C. C. Use an ampersand (&) before the final author's name.

Year:
> Include year of publication.

Title of work: Subtitle of work:
> Italicize the title and capitalize the first word of the title and subtitle and any proper nouns.

Edition:
> Include edition in parentheses if available.

Publisher:
> Do not include the publisher's location.

DOI:
> Include DOI if available using the format https://doi.org/xxxx.xxxx.xxxx.

Example:
Coleman, J. (2001). *Small girl dreaming: The chocolate touch*. Bonnier Books.
Simmons, U. E., & Griffin, A. J. (2019). *Polymer nanotechnology: Nanocomposites* (3rd ed.). John Wiley & Sons.

Edition Other than the First

General Format:	Author, A. A. (Year). *Title of book: Subtitle of book* (Edition). Publisher. DOI
Example:	Powell, I. (2020). *Precision Radiology: Predicting longevity using feature engineering and deep learning methods in a radiomics framework* (4th ed.). Grupo Santillana.

Translation of Book

General Format:	Author, A. A. (Year). *Title of book: Subtitle of book* (A. A. Translator, Trans.). Publisher. (Original work published Year) DOI
Example:	Wood, L. (2021). *Genome engineering* (M. Bennett & G. Barnes, Trans.). Oxford University Press. (Original work published 20018-2019)

Edited Book

General Format:	Author, A. A. (Year). *Title of book: Subtitle of book* (A. A. Editor, Ed.). Publisher. (Original work published Year) DOI
Example:	Bennett, B. (2014). *Methods for evaluating antimicrobial activity* (P. J. C. Hughes, Ed.). Kodansha. (Original work published 1997)

Edited Book (no Author)

General Format:	Editor, A. A. (Ed.). (Year). *Title of book: Subtitle of book.* Publisher. DOI
Example:	Russell, B. V., & James, W. U. (Eds.). (2021). *Binary stars: The key to understanding planetary nebulae.* Springer Nature.

Chapter in an Edited Book

General Format:	Author, A. A. (Year). Title of chapter. In A. A. Editor (Ed.), *Title of book: Subtitle of book* (pp. #-#). Publisher. DOI
Example:	Simmons, X. (2017). Imaging modes of atomic force microscopy. In H. J. Washington & R. Y. Ross (Eds.), *Biology: Application in molecular and cell biology* (pp. 193-198). Cengage Learning.

Multivolume Book

General Format:	Author, A. A. (Year). *Title of book: Subtitle of book* (Edition, Vol. #). Publisher. DOI
Example:	James, S., & Henderson, L. (2021). *Remote carboxylation: Halogenated aliphatic hydrocarbons with carbon dioxide* (12th ed., Vol. H). Macmillan Publishers.

Electronic Book

- If the physical book is published as an eBook or audiobook, it is only necessary to distinguish between the eBook or audiobook and the print version if the content is different:

General Format:
Author, A. A. (Year). *Title of book*. Publisher. URL
Author, A. A. (Year). *Title of book* [eBook edition]. Publisher. URL
Author, A. A. (Year). *Title of book* (A. A. Narrator, Narr.) [Audiobook]. Publisher. URL

5.4 Articles in Periodicals

- For the titles of articles capitalize only:
    o The first letter of the first word of the title and subtitle,
    o The first word after a colon or a dash, and
    o Proper nouns.
- The periodical title is title case and italicized.
- The volume number is also italicized.
- If a DOI (or URL) has been assigned to the article, include it after the page range:
    o Include a DOI even when using the print article.

General Format

General Format:
Author, A. A. (Year). Title of article. *Title of Periodical, Volume*(Issue), pages. DOI

Author, A. A.:
List each author's last name and initial as Author, A. A., Author, B. B., & Author, C. C. Use an ampersand (&) before the final author's name.
Year:
Include year of publication.
Title of article:
Capitalize only first word and proper nouns for the title of article.
***Title of Periodical*:**
Italicize and capitalize each long word in the periodical.
***Volume*:**
Italicize the periodical volume number.
Issue:
If there is an issue number, include it in parentheses, not italicized.
pages:
Include page(s) of the periodical.
DOI:
Include DOI if available using the format https://doi.org/xxxx.xxxx.xxxx.

Example:
Scott, N. S., Reed, E., Evans, T. O., & Thomas, V. (2008). Why some believe that global warming is a hoax. *Green and Sustainable Chemistry, 53(*3), 28–33. https://doi.org/10.1034596/lgk049f-3377

Article in Print Periodical

General Format:	Author, A. A. (Year). Title of article. *Title of Periodical, Volume*(Issue), pages.
Example:	Nelson, Y. (2019). Endangered species. *Graphene, 23*(5), 16–26.

Article in Electronic Periodical

General Format:	Author, A. A. (Year). Title of article. *Title of Periodical, Volume*(Issue), pages. DOI or URL
Example:	Rivera, W., & Mitchell, Q. (2016). The consequences of Brexit for European values. *International Journal of Communications, Network and System Sciences, 9*(6), 19–21. https://doi.org/10.5840/0404959566

Article in Magazine

General Format:	Author, A. A. (Year). Title of article. *Title of Magazine, Volume*(Issue), pages.
Example:	Roberts, C. (2015). How benefits can make your employees happy. *Brain Science, 12*(6), 307–321.

Article in Newspaper

General Format:	Author, A. A. (Year). Title of article. *Title of Newspaper, Volume*(Issue), pages.
Example:	Clark, L. (2021). Taxation aim to small businesses. *The Economy, 14*, 36–39.

Online Scholarly Journal Article

- Provide a DOI, when it is available:
  - If an online scholarly journal article has no DOI and is published online, include the URL instead with the date retrieved.

Online Scholarly Article (with DOI)

General Format:	Author, A. A. (Year). Title of article. *Title of Periodical, Volume*(Issue), pages. DOI
Example:	Williams, N., Morris, O., & Davis, S. F. (2020). How climate has changed. *Journal of Geographic Information System, 55*(13), 14A-14F. https://doi.org/55940.30495/x0495.065

Online Scholarly Article (no DOI)

General Format:	Author, A. A. (Year). Title of article: Subtitle of article. *Database.* Retrieved Month Day, Year, from URL
Example:	Reed, B. (2013). Preventing terrorist attacks. *ScienceOpen.* Retrieved March 21, 2021, from https://www.scienceopen.com/95049/title/005943

- If an online news article is published on the website which is associated with a newspaper:
  - Format the reference entry as article in periodical,
  - Add URL:

General Format:	Author, A. A. (Year, Month Day). Title of article. *Title of Periodical.* URL
Example:	Stewart, K. (1999, March 12). Global citizenship: Pros and cons. *Social Science Research Network.* https://www.social-research-network.com/article/00495.0695

- If an online news article is published on the website which is NOT associated with a newspaper:
  - Italicize the title of the article,
  - Leave the website name unformatted,
  - Add URL:

General Format:	Author, A. A. (Year, Month Day). *Title of article.* Website name. URL
Example:	Rogers, B. (2017, April 4). *Effective time-management for big and small teams.* ALIO. https://www.alio.com/article/titles/44905-6678

Review

General Format:	Author, A. A. (Year). Title of review. [Review of the book *Title of book: Subtitle of book*, by A. A. Author]. *Title of Periodical, Volume*(Issue), pages.
Example:	Cox, U. (2021). Adoption law [Review of the book *Various laws: Abortion around the world*, by Y. U. Gonzalez & C. C. Bailey]. *Building Construction and Planning Research, 41*(2), 35–39.

5.5 Print Sources

Dictionary / Encyclopedia (Group Author)

General Format:	Organization. (Year). Title of entry. In *Title of work* (Edition, pp. #-#). Publisher.
Example:	Longman. (2013). Homeschooling. In *Longman dictionary of contemporary English* (5h ed., pp. 304-305). Longman.

Dictionary / Encyclopedia (Individual Author / Authors)

General Format:	Author, A. A. (Year). Title of entry. In A. A. Editor (ed.), *Title of work* (Edition, pp. #-#). Publisher.
Example:	Bryant, X. G. (2020). Torrenting sites influence creativity and copyright. In H. U. Roberts (ed.), *Concise Oxford English dictionary* (pp. 406-409). Oxford University Press.

Dissertation / Thesis (Abstract)

General Format:	Author, A. A. (Year). Title of dissertation/thesis. *Dissertation Abstracts International, volume*, pages.
Example:	Gray, H. U. (2019). Democracy, education and social change. *Dissertation Abstracts International, 36*(5), 45-47.

Dissertation / Thesis (Published)

General Format:	Author, A. A. (Year). *Title of dissertation/thesis* (Publication No. #) [Type of dissertation/thesis, University]. Database Name.
Example:	Thompson, K. V. (2014). *Effective ways of reducing air pollution* (Publication No. 2350968) [Doctoral dissertation, University of Toronto]. OpenDOAR.

- If the published dissertation or thesis is not published in a database, include the URL to locate the document.

Dissertation / Thesis (Unpublished)

General Format:	Author, A. A. (Year). *Title of dissertation/thesis* [Unpublished Type of dissertation/thesis]. University.
Example:	Cooper, A. S. (2018). *Sexual harassment in the working environment* [Unpublished doctoral dissertation]. University of Chicago.

Report (Individual Author / Authors)

General Format:	Author, A. A. (Year). *Title of report.* Organization Name. URL
Example:	Richardson, M., Baker, H., Jackson, I., & Robinson, O. (2017). *Etsy SEO for vintage sellers 2016.* SEOarts. https://www.seoarts.com/vintage/report/title00349

Government Report (Group Author)

General Format:	Organization. (Year). *Title of report: Subtitle of report.* URL
Example:	United States Foundation for an Ecologically and Socially Just World. (2021). *Report: Self-awareness 2020.* https://www.usf-es.gov/reports/2020/file993039

Brochure

General Format:	Organization. (Year). *Title* [Brochure]. Publisher.
Example:	The Museum of the Future. (2017). *Future architecture* [Brochure]. Museum of Future Publications.

Bible

General Format:	*Bible Version Title.* (Year). Publisher.
Example:	*The English Standard Version Bible.* (2001). Crossway.

5.6 Online Sources

- Electronic citations use square brackets to add specific information.
- Include month and date to the year of publication if possible.
- The label "Retrieved from" is no more in use for URLs or DOIs:
    - Retrieval date may still be used for the sources that are likely to change over the time.

Webpage

General Format:	Author, A. A. (Year, Month Day). *Title of webpage.* Website name. URL
Example:	Evans, U. (2020, May 16). *Eaton 72400-RGH-04 72400 series.* EATON. https://www.eaton.com/tw/en-us/skuPage4.html

- If the source is written by a group of authors (organization), use the name of the group/organization.

General Format:	Organization. (Year, Month Day). *Title of webpage.* Website name. URL
Example:	American Psychological Association. (2020, July 15). *Psychology topics.* APA. https://www.apa.org/topics

- If the author is unknown, use the title instead.
- Include a retrieval date if the source's content is likely to change over the time.

General Format:	*Title of webpage.* (Year, Month Day). Website name. Retrieved Month Date, Year, from URL
Example:	*APA format citation guide.* (2017, August 24). Mendeley. Retrieved March 24, 2021, from https://www.mendeley.com/guides/apa-citation-guide

- If the date of publication is not available, use the abbreviation "n.d." instead.

General Format:	Author, A. A. (n.d.). *Title of webpage.* Website name. URL
Example:	NASA. (n.d.). *Overview: Weather, global warming and climate change.* NASA. https://climate.nasa.gov/resources/glssao

Wikipedia

- Since the Wikipedia articles are likely to change over time, include the URL of archived page of the website:
  - Access the archived version by clicking "View History" and choosing the date/time stamp of the version you use for reference.

General Format:	Title of article. (Year, Month Day). In *Wikipedia*. URL of archived page
Example:	Geology. (2021, March 21). In *Wikipedia*. https://en.wikipedia.org/w/index.php?title=Geology&oldid=1014011568

Dictionary / Encyclopedia (Group Author)

- As long as online dictionary or encyclopedia are continuously updated, use "n.d." for the date of publication and include the retrieval date.

General Format:	Organization. (Year). Title of entry. In *Title of work*. URL
Example:	Macmillan Dictionary. (n.d.). Education. In *Macmillan Dictionary*. Retrieved March 27, 2021, from https://www.macmillan.com.au/dictionary/education

Dictionary / Encyclopedia (Individual Author / Authors)

General Format:	Author, A. A. (Year). Title of entry. In A. A. Editor (Ed.), *Title of work* (edition). Publisher. DOI or URL
Example:	Morris, C. (n.d.). Scholastic. In X. U. Schintler & I. I. McNeely (Eds), *Random house dictionary of the English language*. HarperCollins. https://doi.org/10.3526/gk-5930-00695

Dissertation / Thesis (Database)

General Format:	Author, A. A. (Year). *Title of dissertation/thesis* (Publication No. #) [Type of dissertation/thesis, University]. Database Name.

Example:	Lopez, V. J. (2015). *Political trust and distrust in Japan.* (Publication No. 2349543) [Doctoral dissertation, University of Vancouver]. Public Library of Science.

Data Set

General Format:	Author, A. A. (Year). *Title of dataset* (Version) [Data set]. Publisher. DOI or URL
Example:	Robertson, D. G. (2014). *Population, Australia, 2006-present* (OFPK 22956) [Data set]. Cengage Learning. https://www.cengagedata.edu/article/0059483

Graphic Data

General Format:	Organization. (Year) [Description of graphic data]. Retrieved Month Day, Year, from URL
Example:	Google. (2013). [Google Map of Vancouver port]. Retrieved February 24, 2021, from https://www.google.com/maps/@49.2890976,-123.1111088,17.05z

Computer Software

- Include references only for specialized software:
  - Standard Office software or programming languages should not be cited.

General Format:	Author, A. A. (Year). *Title of software* (Version #). Publisher. URL
Example:	Adobe Acrobat Professional. (2010). *Adobe flash player* (Version 3.7.1). Adobe Acrobat Professional. https://www.adobe.com/ua/products/flashplayer/end-of-life.html

Online Presentation

- For online presentations, provide the file format in square brackets:
  - Word document,
  - PowerPoint slides, etc.

General Format:	Author, A. A. (Year, Month Day). *Title of presentation* [File format]. Publisher. URL
Example:	Roberts, D. (2020, January 16). *Environmental studies* [PowerPoint slides]. Chasings. https://www.chasings.com/presentations/rtitle/00948606

E-Mail

- E-mail is treated as personal communication. Therefore, e-mails are not included in the list of references, but are only cited in the text:

Example:
(E. Robbins, personal communication, February 15, 2021).

Forum

General Format:	Author, A. A. [username]. (Year, Month Day). *Title of post* [Online forum post]. Publisher. URL
Example:	Howard, J. K. [iRmania]. (2015, May 3). *Nonviolence in action* [Online forum post]. Reddit. https://www.reddit.com/s/iRmanA /comments/294503/

Blog Post

General Format:	Author, A. A. (Year, Month Day). Title of post. *Publisher*. URL
Example:	Jenkins, I. (2020, May 26). Remote carboxylation of halogenated aliphatic hydrocarbons with carbon dioxide. *DFG*. https://www.dfg.edu/listtitle/0039485

Facebook Page

General Format:	Author, A. A. (n.d.). *Home* [Facebook page]. Facebook. Retrieved Month Date, Year, from URL
Example:	Nature Calling Global (n.d.). *Home* [Facebook page]. Facebook. Retrieved February 25, 2021 from https://www.facebook.com/naturecalling

Facebook Post

- If the Facebook post includes visuals, indicate type of post in square brackets:
  - Image,
  - Video, etc.

General Format:	Author, A. A. (Year, Month Day). *Text of Facebook post* [Type of post]. Facebook. URL
Example:	Global Trade. (2014, March 30). *Discover a world of trade opportunities in one place with detailed information about imports, market dynamics, tariffs* [Image attached]. Facebook. https://www.facebook.com/GlobalTrade/photos/a.24873-0978-vffj=typeA

Instagram Post

General Format:	Author, A. A. [@username]. (Year, Month Day). *Text of Instagram post* [Type of post]. Instagram. URL
Example:	Bob Jean [@bobjean_9]. (2014, July 21). *Looking back* [Photograph]. Instagram. https://www.instagram.com/p/sdFhngWoAHlvjf/

Twitter Profile

General Format:	Author, A. A. [@username]. (n.d.). *Tweets* [Twitter profile]. Retrieved Month Date, Year, from URL
Example:	Riga News [@riganews]. (n.d.). *Tweets* [Twitter profile]. Retrieved February 27, 2021, from https://twitter.com/riganews

Tweet

- If the tweet includes visuals, indicate type of tweet in square brackets:
  - Tweet,
  - Image,
  - Video, etc.

General Format:	Author, A. A. [@username]. (Year, Month Day). *Text of tweet* [Tweet]. Twitter. URL
Example:	Thompson, U. [@thompdoct_1]. (2018, August 12). *You have got to be kidding...* [Tweet]. Twitter. https://twitter.com/thompdoct_1/status/346082582580

5.7 Audiovisual Sources

"Audiovisual source" refers to any kind of media that contains:
- Audio components,
- Visual components, or
- A combination of both.

Video

- The person who uploaded the video is considered the author.

General Format:	Author, A. A. (Year, Month Day). *Title of video* [Video]. Website name. URL
Example:	Robertson, J. K. (2020, August 25). *What does a geologist do?* [Video]. Geology. https://geology.com/articles/what-is-geology.shtml

YouTube

- If the author's name is different from the YouTube username, include that username in square brackets.

General Format:	Author, A. A. [Username]. (Year, Month Day). *Title of video* [Video]. YouTube. URL
Example:	Gonzales, F. [Korab Lushi]. (2020, April 19). *Two steps from hell* [Video]. YouTube. https://www.youtube.com/watch?v=_FkvjJgl-fkd

TED Talk

General Format:	Author, A. A. (Year, Month Day). *Title of talk* [Video]. TED. URL
Example:	Simmons, L. (2019, September 15). *Letting go of God* [Video]. TED. https://www.ted.com/talks/julia_sweeney_letting_go_of_god

Film

General Format:	Director, A. A. (Director). (Year). *Title of film* [Film]. Production Company.
Example:	Butler, O. (Director). (2015). *The departed* [Film]. Walnut Creek.

Film (Foreign Language)

General Format:	Director, A. A. (Director). (Year). *Title of film in original language* [Translated title of film] [Film]. Production Company.
Example:	Kelly, N. K. (Director). (2006). *Le mépris* [Contempt] [Film]. Encanto Productions.

TV Series

General Format:	Executive Producer, A. A. (Executive Producer). (Year-Year). *Title of series* [TV series]. Production Company.
Example:	Richardson, B. (Executive Producer). (2018-present). *Life on Mars* [TV series]. Warner Bros. Pictures.

TV Series Episode

General Format:	Writer, A. A. (Writer), & Director, A. A. (Director). (Year, Month Day). Title of episode (Season #, Episode #) [Tv series episode]. In A. A. Executive Producer (Executive Producer), *Series title*. Production Company.
Example:	Rodriguez, S. T. (Writer), & Allen, N. V. (Director). (2016, October 3). The mighty Boosh (Season 3, Episode 6) [TV series episode]. In A. Wright & G. Wilson (Executive Producers), *The shadow line*. Lemonlight.

Song / Track

- Recording artist or composer is considered to be the author.

General Format:	Artist, A. A. (Year). Title of song [Song]. On *Title of album* [Album]. Record label.
Example:	Turner, N. (2020). Skins [Song]. On *Leather gang* [Album]. Rip Media Group.

- If the song/track is not included in an album, omit the title of album section.

Music Album

General Format:	Artist, A. A. (Year). *Title of album* [Album]. Record label.
Example:	Brown, F. K. (2020). *Strictly come dancing* [Album]. Island Records.

Podcast

General Format:	Executive Producer, A. A. (Executive Producer). (Year-Year). *Title of podcast* [Audio podcast]. Production Company. URL
Example:	Mitchell, J. (Executive Producer). (2019-present). *Danish political saga* [Audio podcast]. Virgin Records. https://www.newworld-podcast.com/999800

Podcast Episode

General Format:	Executive Producer, A. A. (Executive Producer). (Year, Month Day). Title of podcast episode (No. #) [Audio podcast episode]. In *Title of podcast*. Production Company. URL
Example:	Rivera, H. (Host). (2019, May 18). Six heroes (No. 2) [Audio podcast episode]. In *Insider*. Short Pod Group. https://shortpod-podcast.com/

Image

General Format:	Author, A. A. (Year). *Title of image* [Image]. Website name. URL
Example:	Lewis, A. (2020). *Proof found* [Image]. Borgen. https://borgen.com.au/images/title/0049

Photograph

- If the photograph does not have a title, briefly describe it with your own words and use the description instead of title:
  - Put the description of photograph in square brackets.

General Format:	Photographer, A. A. (Year). Title of photograph [Photograph]. *Publisher*. URL Photographer, A. A. (Year). [Description of photograph] [Photograph]. *Publisher*. URL
Example:	Lee, U. (2021). [Striking men] [Photograph] *The Washington Post*. https://www.washingtonpost.com/article/440395

Museum Artwork

- If the artwork does not have a title, briefly describe the work with your own words and use the description instead of title:
  - Put the description of the artwork in square brackets.

General Format:	Artist, A. A. (Year). Title of artwork [Type of artwork]. Name of Museum, Location. URL Artist, A. A. (Year). [Description of artwork] [Type of artwork]. Name of Museum, Location. URL
Example:	Brown, S. (1980). Twenty minutes a week [Painting]. Museum of London, London, United Kingdom. https://www.museumoflondon.org.uk/museum-london/collection-work-3468070

5.8 Legal Sources

To cite legal materials, APA refers to *Bluebook style in The Bluebook: A Uniform System of Citation, 2015* templates in bibliographies.

Cases and Court Decisions

Cases and court decisions reference entries include:
- Title of case:
  - For example: Collins v. Morris,
- Citation:
  - The volume and page in reporters,
  - Books with published case decisions,
- Jurisdiction of the court:
  - For example: US Supreme Court,
  - For example: U.S. Bankruptcy Court,
- Date of decision,
- URL (optional).

- In-text citations are formatted the same way as any other source:
  - Only court decisions and cases are written in italics for the in-text citations:
    - (*Moore v. Brown,* 1954).

US Supreme Court

General Format:
Name v. Name, Volume U.S. Page (Year). URL

US Circuit Court

General Format:
Name v. Name, Volume F. [or F.2d, F.3d] Page (Year). URL

US District Court

General Format:
Name v. Name, Volume F. Supp. Page (Year). URL

State Court Decision

General Format:
Name v. Name, Volume Reporter Page (Year). URL

- Statute reference entries include:
  - ○ Name of the act,
  - ○ Title, source, and section number of the statute,
  - ○ The publication date,
  - ○ URL (optional).

General Format:
Name of Act, # Source § Section (Year). URL

Legislative Materials

Federal Testimony

General Format:
Title of testimony, ### Cong. (Year) (Testifier Name). URL

- ### Cong. stands for the Congress hearing the testimony:
  - ○ For example: 110th Cong.

Full Federal Hearing

General Format:
Title of hearing, ### Cong. (Year). URL

Unenacted Federal Bill / Resolution

General Format:
Title [if relevant], H.R. or S. bill/resolution number, ### Cong. (Year). URL

- HR and S stand for House of Representatives and Senate.

Enacted Simple / Concurrent Federal Resolution

General Format:
S. Res. ###, ### Cong., Volume Cong. Rec. Page # (Year) (enacted). URL

- Res. ### stands for the resolution number.
- Volume stands for the volume of the Congressional Record.

Federal Report

General Format:
S. (or H.R.) Rep. No. ###-### (Year). URL

- ###-### stands for the report number.

Administrative Materials

Federal Regulation (Codified)

General Format:
Title or Number, Volume C.F.R. § ### (Year). URL

- CFR stands for the Code of Federal Regulations.
- ### stands for the section number.

Federal Regulation (not Codified)

General Format:
Title or Number, Volume F.R. Page (proposed Month Day, Year) (to be codified at Volume C.F.R. § ###). URL

- F.R. stands for the Federal Register.

Executive Order

General Format:
Exec. Order No. #####, 3 C.F.R. Page (Year). URL

Patent

General Format:
Author, A. A. (Year). *Title of patent* (U.S. Patent No. ###). U.S. Patent and Trademark Office. URL

Constitutions, Charters, Treaties, and Conventions

Article of a Constitution

General Format:
U.S. Const. art. ###, § ###.

- ### stands for the article and section numbers.

Amendment to a Constitution

General Format:
U.S. Const. amend. ###

- ### stands for the amendment number.

UN Charter

General Format:
U.N. Charter art. ###, para. ###.

- ### stands for the article and paragraph numbers.

UN Treaty / Convention

General Format:
Name of Treaty or Convention, Month Day, Year, URL

5.9 Other Sources

Interviews

Interviews can be divided into 3 categories:
1. Published interviews,
2. Personal interviews,
3. Research participant interviews.

Published interviews should be included in the reference list:
- For example: newspaper interview,
- For example: magazine interview.

Personal interviews are considered personal communication and are NOT included in the reference list, but are only cited in the text.

Research participant interviews are conducted as part of the research project and are NOT included in the reference list, but are only mentioned in the text.

Published Interview

- For the interview published online, use the format of referencing its medium.

General Format:	Author, A. A. (Year, Month Day). Title of interview. *Title of Periodical, Volume*(Issue), pages. URL
Example:	Brown, P. (1999, June 13). David Lawrence: Domestic gender violence is on the rise. *Intelligent Information Management, 9*(3), 5-7. https://intellgems.com/journal/2134499

- For the audio interview published in a database, treat the interviewee as the author:

General Format:	Author, A. A. (Year, Month Day). *Title of interview* [Interview]. Database. URL
Example:	Scott, U. (2011, July 15). *Evans Robert rare interview* [Interview]. Education Resources Information Center. https://educresor.com/articles/44052056-465

Speech

General Format:	Author, A. A. (Year, Month Day). *Title of speech* [Speech audio recording]. Website Name. URL
Example:	Martin, V. (2020, Dec. 23). *Using animals to conduct research experiments is wrong* [Speech audio recording]. Profit. https://profit.com.au/speech-titanium/678328

Conference Presentation

General Format:	Author, A. A. (Year, Month Day). *Title of presentation* [Type of presentation]. Title of Conference, Location. URL
Example:	Young, X. (2014, Oct. 30). *How has the institution of marriage changed in the postmodern world?* [Conference session]. Marriage Institution 2014 Conference, New York, NY, United States. https://www.youtube.com/watch?v=hjkdfmrRH8G

Large Conference Presentation

General Format:	Author, A. A. (Year, Month Day). Title of contribution. In A. A. Chairperson (Chair), *Title of larger conference* [Type of presentation] Title of Conference, Location. URL
Example:	Thomas, N. H. (2012, Sept. 22). The significance of ethics. In Y. U. Morgan (Chair), *Exploring unfair child labor in the workplace* [Panel presentation] Exploring Workplace 2012, New York, NY, United States.

Conference Proceedings

General Format:	Author, A. A. (Ed.). (Year). *Title of proceedings*. Publisher. URL
Example:	Howard, X., Carter, A., & Taylor, G. (Eds.). (2009). *Proceedings of the 5th annual business conference on a successful startup*. Springer Nature. https://springer-nature.com/titles/dghj3446

Manuscript

General Format:	Author, A. A. (Year). *Title of manuscript.* [Unpublished manuscript / Manuscript in preparation / Manuscript submitted for publication]. Department, University.
Example:	Jackson, V., Hill, R., & Adams, H. (2021). *Various laws on abortion around the world* [Manuscript in preparation]. Department of Medicine, University of Vancouver.

Personal Communication

Personal communication is any kind of communication that cannot be retrieved by a reader:
- Emails,
- Phone conversations, etc.

Personal communications are not included in the reference list:
- Instead, cite personal communications in the text:
  - Include the communicator's name,
  - Add the label "personal communication",
  - Include the date of the communication.

Example:
(I. Torres, personal communication, February 12, 2020).

- For referencing personal communication in a footnote, use the same format:

Example:
[1] K. Peterson (personal communication, March 14, 2021) also claimed that many of her students had difficulties with APA style.

APA manual does not require citing personal communications. However, **it is a good practice** to locate a source if possible.

6.0 QUICK IN-TEXT / REFERENCE LIST EXAMPLES

Book

General Format:	Author, A. A. (Year). *Title of book: Subtitle of book* (Edition). Publisher.
Reference List:	Jackson, H. (2012). *Strategies today: The best strategy to build a house.* Penguin Random House.
In-text Citation:	(Jackson, 2012, p. 34)

E-Book

General Format:	Author, A. A. (Year). *Title of book: Subtitle of book.* Publisher. DOI or URL
Reference List:	Martin, E. (2013). *The house of mirth: Going up.* Hachette Livre. https://amzn.to/V48hdKso
In-text Citation:	(Martin, 2013, paras. 5-8)

Chapter in an Edited Book

General Format:	Author, A. A. (Year). Title of chapter. In A. A. Editor (Ed.), *Title of book: Subtitle of book* (pp. #-#). Publisher. DOI
Reference List:	Thompson, A. (2019). Practical knowledge. In V. Hall & P. Allen (Eds.), *Chasing the time* (pp. 40–52). Simon & Schuster.
In-text Citation:	(Thompson, 2019, p. 43).

Article in Periodical

General Format:	Author, A. A. (Year). Title of article. *Title of Periodical, Volume*(Issue), pages. DOI
Reference List:	Ramirez, B. (2011). Having a powerful headline is important. *Modern Writers Journal, 32*(6), 4–6. https://doi.org/10.35750.30495.4506
In-text Citation:	(Ramirez, 2011)

Webpage

General Format:	Organization. (Year, Month Day). *Title of webpage.* Website name. URL
Reference List:	University of Oxford. (2021, January 20). *Organisation.* University of Oxford. https://www.ox.ac.uk/about/organisation
In-text Citation:	(University of Oxford, 2021)

OR

General Format:	*Title of webpage.* (n.d.). Website name. Retrieved Month Date, Year, from URL
Reference List:	*International Oxford.* (n.d.). University of Oxford. Retrieved February 22, 2021, from https://www.ox.ac.uk/about/international-oxford
In-text Citation:	(*International Oxford*, n.d.)

Dissertation / Thesis

General Format:	Author, A. A. (Year). *Title of dissertation/thesis* (Publication No. #) [Type of dissertation/thesis, University]. Database Name.
Reference List:	Jackson, N. (2010). *Political trust and distrust in Japan* (Publication No. 33992746) [Ph.D dissertation, University of Chicago]. UChicago Dissertations.
In-text Citation:	(Jackson, 2010)

Speech

General Format:	Author, A. A. (Year, Month Day). *Title of speech* [Speech audio recording]. Website Name. URL
Reference List:	Martin, V. (2005, July 12). *Global trade* [Speech audio recording]. Changeover. https://changeover.com/speeches/33399548
In-text Citation:	(Martin, 2005, 03:10)

Dictionary

General Format:	Author, A. A. (Year). Title of entry. In *Title of dictionary* (Edition, p. #). Publisher.
Reference List:	Cambridge University Press. (2020). Irregardless. In *Cambridge advanced learner's dictionary* (4th ed., p. 1029). Cambridge University Press.
In-text Citation:	(Cambridge University Press, 2020)

Film

General Format:	Director, A. A. (Director). (Year). *Title of film* [Film]. Production Company.
Reference List:	Clark, K. (Director). (1990). *Awakenings* [Film]. Parkes/Lasker productions.
In-text Citation:	(Clark, 1990, 01:20:05)

TV Series

General Format:	Writer, A. A. (Writer), & Director, A. A. (Director). (Year, Month Day). Title of episode (Season #, Episode #) [TV series episode]. In A. A. Executive Producer (Executive Producer), *Series title*. Production Company.
Reference List:	Harris, H. (Writer), & Sanchez, A. (Director). (2003, October 3). Victory game (Season 2, Episode 5) [TV series episode]. In H. Allen, B. Walker, V. Nguyen (Executive Producers), *The elephant tonight*. Columbia Pictures Corporation.
In-text Citation:	(Harris et al., 2003)

YouTube Video

General Format:	Author, A. A. [Channel name]. (Year, Month Day). *Title of video* [Video]. YouTube. URL
Reference List:	Jones, E. [National Geographic]. (2015, December 23). *Global Warming 101	National Geographic* [Video]. YouTube. https://www.youtube.com/watch?v=oJAbAT
In-text Citation:	(Jones, 2015)

TED Talk

General Format:	Author, A. A. (Year, Month Day). *Title of talk* [Video]. TED. URL
Reference List:	Adams, C. (2019, May 23). *Possible futures from the intersection of nature, tech and society* [Video]. TED. https://www.ted.com/talks/ intersection_of_nature_tech_and_society
In-text Citation:	(Adams, 2019)

Brochure

General Format:	Organization. (Year). *Title* [Brochure]. Publisher. URL
Reference List:	The Museum of the Future. (2013). *Future architecture* [Brochure]. Museum of Future Publications. http://www.futur-musa.eu/wp-content/3608hdVkld
In-text Citation:	(The Museum of the Future, 2013)

Image

General Format:	Author, A. A. (Year). *Title of work* [Format]. Website name or Museum, Location. URL
Reference List:	Lewis, A. (1901). *Waking up* [Painting]. Museum of London, London, United Kingdom. https://www.museumoflondon.org.uk/museum-london/collection-work-229356040
In-text Citation:	(Lewis, 1901)

Tweet

General Format:	Author, A. A. [@username]. (Year, Month Day). *Text of tweet* [Tweet]. Twitter. URL
Reference List:	Thompson, U. [@thompdoct_1]. (2018, August 12). *You have got to be kidding...* [Tweet]. Twitter. https://twitter.com/thompdoct_1/status/346082768072582580
In-text Citation:	(Thompson, 2018)

Government Report

General Format:	Author, A. A. (Year). *Title of report: Subtitle of report* (Report No. #). Publisher. URL
Reference List:	Young, P. V. (2013). *Protecting the environment: Environmental services passion and commitment* (Report No. CH-BV 305.2). Washington State Department of Transportation. https://www.wsdot.wa.gov/reports/fullreports/305-2.pdf
In-text Citation:	(Young, 2013, p. 33)

Statute

General Format:	Name of Act, # Source § Section (Year). URL
Reference List:	Smuggling Act, 19 U.S.C. §§ 1701-1711 (1976). https://www.loc.gov/item/uscode1976-005019005/
In-text Citation:	(Smuggling Act, 1976)

Court Case

General Format:	Name v. Name, Volume Reporter Page (Court Year). URL
Reference List:	Gibbons v. Ogden, 9 Wheat. 23 (N.Y. Sup. Ct. 1824). https://www.casebriefs.com/blog/law/constitutional-law/constitutional-law-keyed-to-stone/the-powers-of-congress/gibbons-v-ogden-3/
In-text Citation:	(Gibbons v. Ogden, 1824)

Bible

General Format:	*Bible Version Title.* (Year). Publisher. URL
Reference List:	*The English Standard Version Bible.* (2001). Crossway. www.esv.org
In-text Citation:	(*The English Standard Version Bible*, 2001, Genesis 1:1–3

7.0 FOOTNOTES

Footnotes are supplementary details at the bottom of the page. They provide additional information regarding content or copyrights to support the body paragraphs.

There are 2 types of footnotes:
- Content-based footnotes,
- Copyright footnotes.

7.1 Content-Based Footnotes

Content-based footnotes should detail a focused subject:
- Using footnotes to provide additional information enriches the main text.
- Footnotes can also direct readers to alternate sources for more details.

7.2 Copyright Footnotes

When citing commercially published tables, figures, or other data in-text, it is important to credit the copyright information with copyright footnotes:
- Copyright footnotes provide credit to the original source.

7.3 Formatting

Content-Based Footnotes

Footnotes are listed in numerical order of appearance using superscripted numbers:
- There is no space between the callout and superscripted number in the text.
- The superscripted numbers are placed after any punctuation except dashes and parentheses in the text.

- Footnotes can be placed:
  1. At the bottom of the page:
     - Separate the text from the footnotes with a line.
     - List all footnotes (single-spaced).
     - The superscripted numbers are separated from the following text by single space.
  2. On a separate footnotes page after the reference page:
     - Center and bold the label "Footnotes".
     - List all footnotes (double-spaced and indented).

Example:

...

...

...

Liu summarises the main assumption underlying CPTED[1] — namely, that a

modification of the physical environment can lead to a reduction in the crime rate. The work

focuses on applying approved and tested CPTED strategies to the renewal of urban habitats.[2]

The physical causes are identified (that lead to increased crime and fear of crime.[3])

---

[1] Footnotes appear at the bottom of the page.
[2] Footnotes are listed in numerical order of appearance.
[3] Content-based footnotes supplement the part of text they refer to.

Copyright Footnotes

When formatting a copyright footnote:
- Define if the material was fully copied or changed:
    1. Use "From" for directly copied content,
    2. Use "Adapted from" for modified content.
- Include the content's:
    o Title,
    o Author,
    o Year of publication,
    o Source.
- Cite the copyright holder and year of copyright or state whether the source is public domain or licensed under Creative Commons (©).
- If you got permission to reprint the material, indicate that permission was acquired.

8.0 APPENDICES

An appendix (or "appendices") may be included to allow readers better understand the material in case there is a need to provide additional content that may not fit within the main text of paper.

An appendix can include following:
- Transcripts of conducted interviews (quoted in the text).
- Documents, such as questionnaires, tests, or results, etc.
- Detailed statistical data.

Therefore, there are 2 main types of appendices:
1. Text appendix,
2. Table/figure appendix.

Each appendix must be referred to at least once in the text.

8.1 Formatting Appendices

- An appendix should be created on a separate page after references and footnotes:
  - Label "Appendix" is:
    - At the top of the page,
    - Centered, bolded, and written in title case.
  - Label "Appendix" is followed by a title on the next line:
    - Centered,
    - Describes the subject of the appendix.
- If there are several appendices, each appendix should be labeled with a capital letter:
  - For example: Appendix A, Appendix B, Appendix C, etc.

Example:

Appendix A

Subject of the Appendix

8.2 Text Appendices

- Text appendices should be formatted in traditional paragraph style.
- Beside text itself, text appendices may still include visuals, such as:
  - Tables and figures,
  - Equations, etc.
- All visuals should be named starting with the letter of the corresponding appendix and number:
  - For example, in text Appendix A with one table, the table should be labeled "Table A1".
  - For example, in text Appendix B with one table and two figures, the table should be labeled "Table B1" and figures should be labeled "Figure B1" and "Figure B2".

8.3 Table and/or Figure Appendices

Table appendix or figure appendix solely contain a table or a figure respectively:
- The title of the table or figure should be replaced with the title of the corresponding appendix:
  - For example, in table Appendix A (which only includes one table), the table should be labeled "Appendix A" instead of "Table A1".

9.0 APA SAMPLE PAPER

The APA Manual (7th edition) determines different formatting requirements for student and professional papers:
1.   Papers for credit in a course,
2.   Papers for scholarly publication.

These requirements mostly refer to the cover page and running head. Significantly, citation standards do not vary between the two types of paper.

For your benefit, we have given two versions of APA sample paper:
1.   Student paper,
2.   Professional paper.

1. Student Paper

Modern Period in the English Literature:

Key Points about Modern Period

Marcus White

Department of English Literature, Heldens University

ELD 1201: Modern English Literature

Dr. Korsh

April 25, 2021

NEW PAGE:

Abstract

Lorem ipsum dolor sit amet, consectetur adipiscing elit. Vivamus id dapibus libero. Phasellus vel urna nisi. Orci varius natoque penatibus et magnis dis parturient montes, nascetur ridiculus mus. Curabitur ac luctus nisi, sed maximus nibh. Curabitur congue accumsan nisi, a sollicitudin turpis aliquam at. Phasellus suscipit est eget augue sagittis, ac lobortis ex egestas. Mauris vitae purus lacus. Proin imperdiet feugiat posuere. Sed a lacus aliquam, cursus sem et, faucibus nibh. Nulla diam diam, aliquam ac ante ac, blandit ultricies lectus. Sed vitae enim nisl. Praesent eu erat eget enim viverra sagittis. Nunc vel lacinia dolor, in fermentum neque. Donec consequat rutrum quam. Duis eget lacus mollis, gravida risus eu, auctor lorem. Donec sit amet libero nisi. Pellentesque sit amet ante rutrum, feugiat ipsum vel, ornare leo. Proin tincidunt purus ut massa aliquam, fermentum malesuada elit interdum. Sed posuere ut mauris non molestie. Integer nec condimentum mi, nec ornare nisi. Nulla non sagittis nibh. Suspendisse in felis at ipsum tristique pharetra sed in neque. Cras orci purus, pulvinar non placerat id, dapibus sed felis.

Keywords: Ipsum, purus, pulvinar

NEW PAGE:

Modern Period in the English Literature: Key Points about Modern Period

Lorem ipsum dolor sit amet, consectetur adipiscing elit. Vivamus orci quam, iaculis faucibus risus eget, lobortis tempor ligula. Aliquam eu diam maximus, iaculis libero aliquet, volutpat nisi. Praesent nunc lorem, sodales a viverra a, placerat id leo. Praesent rutrum facilisis velit, vitae sodales eros aliquam sit amet. Lorem ipsum dolor sit amet, consectetur adipiscing elit, ligula nunc porta est, interdum pellentesque sem ligula at sapien (Harris et al., 2003). Vestibulum eu nisl erat. Cras finibus a est ac suscipit. Nullam pretium lectus nec eros dapibus, vitae laoreet ante condimentum. Donec eget efficitur ligula. Duis sed tincidunt eros, ac porttitor velit. In hac habitasse platea dictumst.

Heading (Level 1)

Nulla eu velit vestibulum, mattis nunc a, pretium metus. Vestibulum nec metus quis sem fermentum cursus. Nulla eleifend ante venenatis, placerat massa nec, dictum odio. Sed non aliquam mauris. Donec eget arcu euismod, tempor eros non, consectetur lorem.[1] Fusce ullamcorper sem ligula, sed sagittis eros gravida sed (Ramirez, 2011). Donec convallis malesuada nibh sodales suscipit. Cras molestie, arcu ac.

Heading (Level 2)

Cras at diam hendrerit, accumsan urna pharetra, rutrum ipsum. Ut pharetra, purus in finibus elementum, sit amet sagittis elit semper ac. Nullam interdum iaculis elit vel ultricies. Pellentesque vel magna nulla nisi malesuada magna, quis elementum tellus arcu sit amet urna. Proin volutpat lectus non nisi aliquam venenatis. In dictum nisl eget purus posuere, eget ornare dui sit amet sagittis elit semper ac. Nullam interdum iaculis elit vel ultricies. Pellentesque vel mag vitae sodales eros aliquam sit amet. Lorem ipsum

---

[1] K. Peterson (personal communication, March 14, 2021) also claimed that many of her students had difficulties with APA style.

NEW PAGE:

dictum. Curabitur tempus nisl sapien, ac vehicula est auctor ac. Integer iaculis nunc at risus viverra, non tincidunt nulla lobortis.

Heading (Level 3)

Praesent vestibulum sem non dictum aliquet. Donec nec dictum lacus, eu imperdiet turpis. Donec tincidunt semper sapien ut auctor. Aenean ornare ullamcorper risus a euismod. Donec maximus iaculis mi dignissim ultricies (Young, 2013, p. 33). Pellentesque imperdiet finibus neque in convallis. Vestibulum interdum euismod libero. Aliquam porttitor auctor porttitor. Pellentesque eget tortor vitae ligula accumsan semper.

Heading (Level 3)

Vivamus iaculis massa metus, at ultricies quam feugiat fermentum. Praesent placerat posuere nulla in tempor. Sed ut elit eros. Quisque. Praesent accumsan enim orci, non vehicula lorem tristique ac. Suspendisse potenti. Nunc blandit fermentum dui eget egestas. Quisque in (I. Torres, personal communication, February 12, 2020). Fusce tincidunt ornare orci, sit amet sagittis elit semper ac. Nullam interdum iaculis elit vel ultricies. Pellentesque vel magna non quam imperdiet eleifend sed tristique ligula. In eget ligula vel magna sodales fermentum nec ac nisi. Etiam dictum tincidunt libero eget rutrum. Integer ac orci quis sem sagittis vestibulum. Vestibulum ante ipsum primis in faucibus orci luctus et ultrices posuere cubilia curae.

Aliquam erat volutpat (Adams, 2019). Suspendisse erat sem, eleifend vitae ipsum vitae, auctor bibendum nunc. Suspendisse at tortor scelerisque, gravida quam ut, tincidunt massa. Quisque fermentum est justo. Vestibulum consectetur velit quis congue consectetur. Donec sed ante odio. Ut maximus enim eu felis venenatis, nec faucibus augue venenatis. Praesent finibus velit et fermentum est justo quam imperdiet eleifend sit amet sagittis elit semper ac. Nullam interdum iaculis elit vel ultricies. Pellentesque vel

5

convallis hendrerit. Ut lobortis suscipit massa, eu scelerisque tellus sollicitudin vel.

Donec viverra elit nec lectus feugiat, vitae vehicula odio faucibus.

Table 1

Title of Table Title Case

Stub Heading	Column Spanner 1		Column Spanner 2	
	Column Heading 1	Column Heading 2	Column Heading 3	Column Heading 4
	Table Spanner 1			
Row 1	XXX	XXX[a]	XXX	XXX
Row 2	XXX	XXX	XXX	XXX
	Table Spanner 2			
Row 3	XXX	XXX	XXX***	XXX
Row 4	XXX	XXX	XXX***	XXX

Note. A general note.

[a]A specific note.

***A probability note.

Quisque purus mi, congue at facilisis et, blandit nec nulla. Integer molestie hendrerit mauris, vitae euismod metus lobortis et. Donec sapien sem, tempus ut lobortis a, ullamcorper et nibh. Thompson offered rras pulvinar eros a sapien fermentum facilisis aliquam ullamcorper ante mauris, sed condimentum eros convallis id (2018). Donec at nulla enim. Praesent turpis nisl, cursus ac arcu in, rhoncus pharetra elit. Pellentesque suscipit auctor arcu. Sed id erat purus.

Heading (Level 2)

Curabitur vel eros porta, imperdiet erat et, venenatis ante. Sed convallis nulla quis sem dapibus scelerisque. Nulla facilisi. Ut ultrices ut leo ut elementum. Vestibulum imperdiet ultricies hendrerit mauris, vitae euismod metus lobortis et. Donec sapien sem dignissim volutpat mauris, eget tincidunt quam molestie aliquam. Aliquam diam est, porttitor ac enim sit amet, placerat pretium purus. Quisque eleifend auctor neque, sit amet fermentum elit tempus at.

Heading (Level 1)

Quisque tristique vehicula sapien posuere posuere. In maximus nisi sit amet diam dignissim commodo. Praesent condimentum turpis bibendum, molestie odio eget, convallis nisi. Duis faucibus diam non lectus iaculis, sed semper nunc elementum. Fusce iaculis, elit non porttitor faucibus, nibh arcu porttitor eros, sed suscipit nulla neque sit amet lacus. In hac habitasse platea dictumst. Cras et suscipit urna. Etiam volutpat odio (Smuggling Act, 1976). Vel lectus tristique luctus. Donec id hendrerit risus. Donec interdum turpis sit amet ligula porttitor, sit amet gravida lacus hendrerit. Aenean dignissim, tellus placerat imperdiet venenatis, ipsum odio varius eros, quis elementum quam mi id ligula. Donec tristique vehicula sapien ut molestie. Duis rutrum dapibus dui, eu aliquam erat (Martin, 2013, paras. 5-8).

Pellentesque imperdiet diam ligula, aliquam laoreet ante faucibus ut. Duis diam lectus, malesuada non sollicitudin id, pellentesque at diam. Phasellus convallis urna eget augue ullamcorper fringilla. Aenean varius eros a nibh sagittis, id mattis diam rhoncus. Vestibulum maximus tincidunt metus ac congue.

NEW PAGE:

References

Adams, C. (2019, May 23). *Possible futures from the intersection of nature, tech and society* [Video]. TED. https://www.ted.com/talks/possible_futures_from_the_intersection_of_nature_tech_and_society

Bennett, B. (2014). *Methods for evaluating antimicrobial activity* (P. J. C. Hughes, Ed.). Kodansha. (Original work published 1997)

Brown, P. (1999, June 13). David Lawrence: Domestic gender violence is on the rise. *Intelligent Information Management, 9*(3), 5-7. https://intellgems.com/journal/2134499

Clark, K. (Director). (1990). *Awakenings* [Film]. Parkes/Lasker productions.

Coleman, J. (2001). *Small girl dreaming: The chocolate touch.* Bonnier Books.

Google. (2013). [Google Map of Vancouver port]. Retrieved February 24, 2021, from https://www.google.com/maps/@49.2890976,-123.1111088,17.05z

Green, A., Collins, F., Wright, D., Collins, H., Miller, B., Reed, G., Morgan, F. L., Green, V., Anderson, C., Adams, D., Li, Q., Scott, R., Hernandez, T. K., Walker, C., Baker, A. K., Evans, T. T. R., Morris, B. O., Brown, B., White, M., . . . Murphy, E. K. (2010). Molecular mechanisms underlying the evolution of the signalosome. *Science Advances, 54*(7), 22-26. http://dx.doi.org/1544.3463.4540/drky77

Jackson, V., Hill, R., & Adams, H. (2021). *Various laws on abortion around the world* [Manuscript in preparation]. Department of Medicine, University of Vancouver.

NEW PAGE:

Phillips, V. C., Campbell, S., Johnson, F. T., Hall, T. Y., & Lopez, H. (2017). The

Rohingya people of Myanmar: Health, human rights, and identity.

International Journal of Clean Coal and Energy, 56(8), 23-31.

Phillips, V. C., Rogers, F. L., Green, T. D., Baker, V., & Harris, D. D. (2017). Charting

organellar importomes by quantitative mass spectrometry. *International*

Journal of Geosciences, 1(2), 34-56.

Richardson, B. (Executive Producer). (2018-present). *Life on Mars* [TV series]. Warner

Bros. Pictures.

Rivera, H. (Host). (2019, May 18). Six heroes (No. 2) [Audio podcast episode]. In

Insider. Short Pod Group. https://shortpod-podcast.com/

Robertson, J. K. (2020, August 25). *What does a geologist do?* [Video]. Geology.

https://geology.com/articles/what-is-geology.shtml

Wright, F. R. (2015a). Branched-chain and aromatic amino acids in relation to

behavioral problems among young Inuit from Nunavik, Canada: A cohort

study. *International Journal of Organic Chemistry, 7*(6), 8-12.

Wright, F. R. (2015b). Chemokine profiles of interstitial pneumonia in patients with

dermatomyositis: A case control study. *International Journal of Medical*

Physics, Clinical Engineering and Radiation Oncology, 12(5), 6-7.

Note: This is a sample reference list. For the purpose of demonstrating a number of

references, this list contains references that do not match in-text citations in

the paper. Please note that in a real paper all references should match in-text

citations and vice versa.

NEW PAGE:

Appendix

Title of Figure Title Case

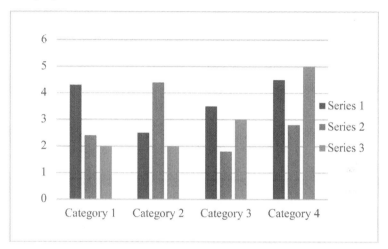

Note. General note explaining units of measurement, abbreviations, etc. or provide

citation information.

2. Professional Paper

Modern Period in the English Literature:

Key Points about Modern Period

Marcus White and White Andrew

English Literature Online Lab

Department of English Literature, Heldens University

Author Note

Marcus White ⬤ https://orcid.org/1257-8436-2456

White Andrew ⬤ https://orcid.org/4678-8926-3324

White Andrew is now at the Department of English History, Heldens University.

We have no conflicts of interests to disclose.

Correspondence concerning this article should be addressed to White Andrew, 34 E New Heldens St., North Hollick KB 302928. Email: whiteandrew@heldens.edu

NEW PAGE:

Abstract

Lorem ipsum dolor sit amet, consectetur adipiscing elit. Vivamus id dapibus libero. Phasellus vel urna nisi. Orci varius natoque penatibus et magnis dis parturient montes, nascetur ridiculus mus. Curabitur ac luctus nisi, sed maximus nibh. Curabitur congue accumsan nisi, a sollicitudin turpis aliquam at. Phasellus suscipit est eget augue sagittis, ac lobortis ex egestas. Mauris vitae purus lacus. Proin imperdiet feugiat posuere. Sed a lacus aliquam, cursus sem et, faucibus nibh. Nulla diam diam, aliquam ac ante ac, blandit ultricies lectus. Sed vitae enim nisl. Praesent eu erat eget enim viverra sagittis. Nunc vel lacinia dolor, in fermentum neque. Donec consequat rutrum quam. Duis eget lacus mollis, gravida risus eu, auctor lorem. Donec sit amet libero nisi. Pellentesque sit amet ante rutrum, feugiat ipsum vel, ornare leo. Proin tincidunt purus ut massa aliquam, fermentum malesuada elit interdum. Sed posuere ut mauris non molestie. Integer nec condimentum mi, nec ornare nisi. Nulla non sagittis nibh. Suspendisse in felis at ipsum tristique pharetra sed in neque. Cras orci purus, pulvinar non placerat id, dapibus sed felis.

Keywords: Ipsum, purus, pulvinar

NEW PAGE:

Modern Period in the English Literature: Key Points about Modern Period

Lorem ipsum dolor sit amet, consectetur adipiscing elit. Vivamus orci quam, iaculis faucibus risus eget, lobortis tempor ligula. Aliquam eu diam maximus, iaculis libero aliquet, volutpat nisi. Praesent nunc lorem, sodales a viverra a, placerat id leo. Praesent rutrum facilisis velit, vitae sodales eros aliquam sit amet. Lorem ipsum dolor sit amet, consectetur adipiscing elit, ligula nunc porta est, interdum pellentesque sem ligula at sapien (Harris et al., 2003). Vestibulum eu nisl erat. Cras finibus a est ac suscipit. Nullam pretium lectus nec eros dapibus, vitae laoreet ante condimentum. Donec eget efficitur ligula. Duis sed tincidunt eros, ac porttitor velit. In hac habitasse platea dictumst.

Heading (Level 1)

Nulla eu velit vestibulum, mattis nunc a, pretium metus. Vestibulum nec metus quis sem fermentum cursus. Nulla eleifend ante venenatis, placerat massa nec, dictum odio. Sed non aliquam mauris. Donec eget arcu euismod, tempor eros non, consectetur lorem.[1] Fusce ullamcorper sem ligula, sed sagittis eros gravida sed (Ramirez, 2011). Donec convallis malesuada nibh sodales suscipit. Cras molestie, arcu ac.

Heading (Level 2)

Cras at diam hendrerit, accumsan urna pharetra, rutrum ipsum. Ut pharetra, purus in finibus elementum, nulla nisi malesuada magna, quis elementum tellus arcu sit amet urna. Proin volutpat lectus non nisi aliquam venenatis. In dictum nisl eget purus posuere, eget ornare dui lobortis tempor ligula. Aliquam eu diam maximus, iaculis libero aliquet, volutpat nisi. Praesent nunc lorem aliquam mauris. Donec eget arcu euismod,

---

[1] K. Peterson (personal communication, March 14, 2021) also claimed that many of her students had difficulties with APA style.

NEW PAGE:

dictum. Curabitur tempus nisl sapien, ac vehicula est auctor ac. Integer iaculis nunc at risus viverra, non tincidunt nulla lobortis.

Heading (Level 3)

Praesent vestibulum sem non dictum aliquet. Donec nec dictum lacus, eu imperdiet turpis. Donec tincidunt semper sapien ut auctor. Aenean ornare ullamcorper risus a euismod. Donec maximus iaculis mi dignissim ultricies (Young, 2013, p. 33). Pellentesque imperdiet finibus neque in convallis. Vestibulum interdum euismod libero. Aliquam porttitor auctor porttitor. Pellentesque eget tortor vitae ligula accumsan semper.

Heading (Level 3)

Vivamus iaculis massa metus, at ultricies quam feugiat fermentum. Praesent placerat posuere nulla in tempor. Sed ut elit eros. Quisque. Praesent accumsan enim orci, non vehicula lorem tristique ac. Suspendisse potenti. Nunc blandit fermentum dui eget egestas. Quisque in (I. Torres, personal communication, February 12, 2020). Fusce tincidunt ornare orci, sit amet sagittis elit semper ac. Nullam interdum iaculis elit vel ultricies. Pellentesque vel magna non quam imperdiet eleifend sed tristique ligula. In eget ligula vel magna sodales fermentum nec ac nisi. Etiam dictum tincidunt libero eget rutrum. Integer ac orci quis sem sagittis vestibulum. Vestibulum ante ipsum primis in faucibus orci luctus et ultrices posuere cubilia curae.

Aliquam erat volutpat (Adams, 2019). Suspendisse erat sem, eleifend vitae ipsum vitae, auctor bibendum nunc. Suspendisse at tortor scelerisque, gravida quam ut, tincidunt massa. Quisque fermentum est justo. Vestibulum consectetur velit quis congue consectetur. Donec sed ante odio. Ut maximus enim eu felis venenatis, nec faucibus augue venenatis. Praesent finibus velit et sit amet sagittis elit semper ac. Nullam inter

NEW PAGE:

convallis hendrerit. Ut lobortis suscipit massa, eu scelerisque tellus sollicitudin vel.

Donec viverra elit nec lectus feugiat, vitae vehicula odio faucibus.

Table 1

Title of Table Title Case

Stub Heading	Column Spanner 1		Column Spanner 2	
	Column Heading 1	Column Heading 2	Column Heading 3	Column Heading 4
Table Spanner 1				
Row 1	XXX	XXX[a]	XXX	XXX
Row 2	XXX	XXX	XXX	XXX
Table Spanner 2				
Row 3	XXX	XXX	XXX***	XXX
Row 4	XXX	XXX	XXX***	XXX

Note. A general note.

[a]A specific note.

***A probability note.

Quisque purus mi, congue at facilisis et, blandit nec nulla. Integer molestie

hendrerit mauris, vitae euismod metus lobortis et. Donec sapien sem, tempus ut lobortis

a, ullamcorper et nibh. Thompson offered rras pulvinar eros a sapien fermentum facilisis

aliquam ullamcorper ante mauris, sed condimentum eros convallis id (2018). Donec at

nulla enim. Praesent turpis nisl, cursus ac arcu in, rhoncus pharetra elit. Pellentesque

suscipit auctor arcu. Sed id erat purus.

Heading (Level 2)

Curabitur vel eros porta, imperdiet erat et, venenatis ante. Sed convallis nulla

quis sem dapibus scelerisque. Nulla facilisi. Ut ultrices ut leo ut elementum. Vestibulum

NEW PAGE:

dignissim volutpat mauris, eget tincidunt quam molestie aliquam. Aliquam diam est, porttitor ac enim sit amet, placerat pretium purus. Quisque eleifend auctor neque, sit amet fermentum elit tempus at.

Heading (Level 1)

Quisque tristique vehicula sapien posuere posuere. In maximus nisi sit amet diam dignissim commodo. Praesent condimentum turpis bibendum, molestie odio eget, convallis nisi. Duis faucibus diam non lectus iaculis, sed semper nunc elementum. Fusce iaculis, elit non porttitor faucibus, nibh arcu porttitor eros, sed suscipit nulla neque sit amet lacus. In hac habitasse platea dictumst. Cras et suscipit urna. Etiam volutpat odio (Smuggling Act, 1976). Vel lectus tristique luctus. Donec id hendrerit risus. Donec interdum turpis sit amet ligula porttitor, sit amet gravida lacus hendrerit. Aenean dignissim, tellus placerat imperdiet venenatis, ipsum odio varius eros, quis elementum quam mi id ligula. Donec tristique vehicula sapien ut molestie. Duis rutrum dapibus dui, eu aliquam erat (Martin, 2013, paras. 5-8).

Pellentesque imperdiet diam ligula, aliquam laoreet ante faucibus ut. Duis diam lectus, malesuada non sollicitudin id, pellentesque at diam. Phasellus convallis urna eget augue ullamcorper fringilla. Aenean varius eros a nibh sagittis, id mattis diam rhoncus. Vestibulum maximus tincidunt metus ac congue.

NEW PAGE:

References

Adams, C. (2019, May 23). *Possible futures from the intersection of nature, tech and society* [Video]. TED. https://www.ted.com/talks/possible_futures_from_the_intersection_of_nature_tech_and_society

Bennett, B. (2014). *Methods for evaluating antimicrobial activity* (P. J. C. Hughes, Ed.). Kodansha. (Original work published 1997)

Brown, P. (1999, June 13). David Lawrence: Domestic gender violence is on the rise. *Intelligent Information Management, 9*(3), 5-7. https://intellgems.com/journal/2134499

Clark, K. (Director). (1990). *Awakenings* [Film]. Parkes/Lasker productions.

Coleman, J. (2001). *Small girl dreaming: The chocolate touch*. Bonnier Books.

Google. (2013). [Google Map of Vancouver port]. Retrieved February 24, 2021, from https://www.google.com/maps/@49.2890976,-123.1111088,17.05z

Green, A., Collins, F., Wright, D., Collins, H., Miller, B., Reed, G., Morgan, F. L., Green, V., Anderson, C., Adams, D., Li, Q., Scott, R., Hernandez, T. K., Walker, C., Baker, A. K., Evans, T. T. R., Morris, B. O., Brown, B., White, M., . . . Murphy, E. K. (2010). Molecular mechanisms underlying the evolution of the signalosome. *Science Advances, 54*(7), 22-26. http://dx.doi.org/1544.3463.4540/drky77

Jackson, V., Hill, R., & Adams, H. (2021). *Various laws on abortion around the world* [Manuscript in preparation]. Department of Medicine, University of Vancouver.

NEW PAGE:

Phillips, V. C., Campbell, S., Johnson, F. T., Hall, T. Y., & Lopez, H. (2017). The
Rohingya people of Myanmar: Health, human rights, and identity.
International Journal of Clean Coal and Energy, 56(8), 23-31.

Phillips, V. C., Rogers, F. L., Green, T. D., Baker, V., & Harris, D. D. (2017). Charting
organellar importomes by quantitative mass spectrometry. *International
Journal of Geosciences, 1*(2), 34-56.

Richardson, B. (Executive Producer). (2018-present). *Life on Mars* [TV series]. Warner
Bros. Pictures.

Rivera, H. (Host). (2019, May 18). Six heroes (No. 2) [Audio podcast episode]. In
Insider. Short Pod Group. https://shortpod-podcast.com/

Robertson, J. K. (2020, August 25). *What does a geologist do?* [Video]. Geology.
https://geology.com/articles/what-is-geology.shtml

Wright, F. R. (2015a). Branched-chain and aromatic amino acids in relation to
behavioral problems among young Inuit from Nunavik, Canada: A cohort
study. *International Journal of Organic Chemistry, 7*(6), 8-12.

Wright, F. R. (2015b). Chemokine profiles of interstitial pneumonia in patients with
dermatomyositis: A case control study. *International Journal of Medical
Physics, Clinical Engineering and Radiation Oncology, 12*(5), 6-7.

Note: This is a sample reference list. For the purpose of demonstrating a number of
references, this list contains references that do not match in-text citations in
the paper. Please note that in a real paper all references should match in-text
citations and vice versa.

NEW PAGE:

Appendix

Title of Figure Title Case

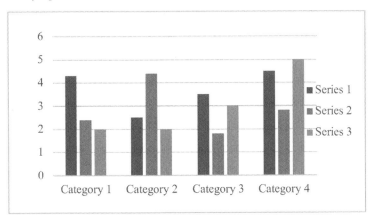

Note. General note explaining units of measurement, abbreviations, etc. or provide

citation information.

SOURCES

Since the 7th edition of the APA manual is a new release, there are fewer supplementary resources than for the 6th edition.

American Psychological Association offers following online resources:

- APA Style Website: https://apastyle.apa.org,
- APA 7 Reference Guide (PDF): https://apastyle.apa.org/instructional-aids/reference-guide.pdf,
- APA 7 Supplemental Resources: https://apastyle.apa.org/products/supplemental-resources.

For detailed APA standards and procedures, consult the *Publication Manual of the American Psychological Association* (7th edition).

Additional Print Resources

Detailed information on APA style is available in a variety of print distributions. A large number of these resources may be accessible at Campus libraries:

- Publication Manual of the American Psychological Association (7th edition):
  - ISBN 10: 143383216X,
  - ISBN 13: 978-1433832161.
- Concise Guide to APA Style (7th edition):
  - ISBN 10: 1433832739,
  - ISBN 13: 978-1433832734.

In case you are using APA style for a class assignment, please counsel your instructor for assistance with using APA style.

Your instructor is the final authority on how to properly apply APA style guidelines in your specific case.

FREE **APA "In-Text Citations & Reference List" Tables** from the author are available at: https://appearancepublishers.wordpress.com/apa-manual-made-easy/

CHECK MORE BOOKS
on Amazon

https://www.amazon.com/Appearance-Publishers/e/B091TLWPW9

APA 7th Manual Made Easy

MLA Handbook 9th Edition Simplified

https://www.amazon.com/gp/product/B091SMVWKN/

https://www.amazon.com/gp/product/B092MY8YWT/

APA 7th Quick Study Guidelines in Tables

Strong Verbs Thesaurus for Fiction Writers

https://www.amazon.com/gp/product/B0938D4QR4

https://www.amazon.com/gp/product/B0933KSDSD